The Elements of Heraldry

CONTAINING

AN EXPLANATION OF THE PRINCIPLES OF THE SCIENCE
AND A GLOSSARY OF THE TECHNICAL
TERMS EMPLOYED

AND

WITH AN ESSAY UPON THE USE OF COAT-ARMOR
IN THE UNITED STATES

BY

WILLIAM H. WHITMORE

WEATHERVANE BOOKS • NEW YORK

TABLE OF CONTENTS

TABLE OF CONTENTS.

PART IV.

APPENDIX.

PUBLISHER'S FOREWORD

IN order to add to the ever growing list of source books of genealogical material, we feel it is important to discover and publish volumes long out of print.

Such a book is *Elements of Heraldry*. First published in 1866, it was prepared expressly for the American public. At that time, heraldry was enjoying a great popular revival in the United States. But the only available material pertained exclusively to the fine details of British heraldry and did not provide the background information sought by interested Americans. *Elements of Heraldry* attempted to fill the gap by clearly setting forth the basics of heraldic design and terminology.

In reissuing this book we are pleased to make available additional research material for the genealogical scholar. This book was originally published in 1866 by Lee and Shepard, of Boston.

PREFACE

WORD of explanation may be expected on the appearance of the first treatise on Heraldry prepared for the American public. The cause of its publication is this: In January, 1865, the Committee on Heraldry, appointed by the New-England Historic-Genealogical Society, decided to commence the publication of all the existing specimens of coats-of-arms used here prior to the Revolution. Meeting a sufficient response from those interested in Genealogy, it was soon evident that there was a great want of information on the general subject of Heraldry.

It was supposed that this could be supplied by the republication of some one of the numerous manuals or text-books issued in England. On examination it was found that this was impracticable, since the smaller works were badly arranged and full of antiquated errors, while the larger manuals contained an infinite amount of matter only remotely connected with Heraldry.

Under these circumstances there seemed to be but one course open, — to prepare such a compilation as should teach the reader all the essential parts of the science, and should present them within a reasonable compass. Of course, as there were no new principles to be discovered, the only merit of such a work must lie in the clearness of its method, and its adaptation to the wants of American readers. The leading authorities have been carefully studied, and, it is believed, have been faithfully reproduced.

The compiler hopes that any defects discoverable will be excused, in consideration of the difficulty of perfect accuracy in a pioneer work. Although, some years since, a little book entitled "A Handbook of Heraldry" was published by T. W. Gwilt Mapleson, Esq., it was of so trivial a character that this must be regarded as the first attempt to gather out that portion of the description of Heraldry which will be especially useful on this side of the Atlantic.

BOSTON, May 28, 1866.

INTRODUCTION

ERALDRY is a science which treats of the classi-
fication and description of certain hereditary emblems, and the rules which govern their use. This
system can be traced to the beginning of the
thirteenth century, and with various modifications
has been in use in nearly every European country. In the following treatise it will be shown, that, by certain easy rules, a
system of emblems has been formed, capable of almost infinite
expansion, and yet susceptible of easy comprehension.

It would be useless to speak of the extensive employment
formerly made of these devices : the traveller abroad meets the
evidences at every step. Aside from the important position
which the science holds in Architecture, it has become one of
the most influential means of forming modern society abroad.

Although, during the period when these States were English
colonies, the use of coats-of-arms was sufficiently common, its
total disuse during the present century has led to a complete
ignorance of the whole subject here. Within a few years, coats-
of-arms have indeed been profusely assumed, but with such a
total disregard of all authority as to prove the ignorance even of
that part of the community which ought to have been better

instructed. The ordinary mode of assuming armorial bearings has been a reference to the nearest seal-engraver, who, from some heraldic Encyclopædia, has furnished the applicant with the arms of any family of the same name.

To strike at the root of this evil, it is necessary to state, in the most explicit manner, that there is no such thing as a coat-of-arms belonging to the bearers of any particular surname.

Competent writers have already disabused the public mind of the idea that identity of name argues identity of origin. No one now supposes, that all Browns or Joneses or Smiths or Robinsons trace their descent from one man, the original assumer of the name. Still, it has been much more difficult to convince a Brown, Jones, Smith, or Robinson, that he was not entitled to a coat-of-arms "belonging to his name."

Examination will soon convince us that this idea is totally unfounded. The first assumer or grantee of a coat-of-arms took that as his own distinguishing mark. It became hereditary in his own family; but his namesakes, or even relatives, have no claim to share it with him.

It follows, therefore, that whoever uses a coat-of-arms, by that act proclaims his lineal descent from the person who first assumed it. It is useless to attempt any evasion of this fact. However true it may be that even in England the law does not interpose, we ought, in this country, from the very absence of law, to exercise a wise restraint. The sole value or interest of our American coats-of-arms consists in the remembrance of an honorable ancestry. We cannot afford to insult our real progenitors by a false claim to others.

Coats-of-arms were frequently used in New England during the Colonial period; and, though we can speak only of this section from actual knowledge, it is most probable that they were used in the rest of the original thirteen colonies. These arms are worthy of preservation, since they are valuable evidence for the genealogist. At the date when they were used, the English rules were in force here. The time since the settlement of the country was not so long as to forbid the acceptance of tradition as evidence. We may believe that those who displayed armorial insignia had good grounds for the adoption.

To the general community of readers, however, the following treatise is offered on different grounds. The science itself is one of which no educated person should be entirely ignorant. Many of the terms of heraldry have become familiar expressions; many of the best English authors employ words which are intelligible only to those acquainted with the rudiments at least of this science. Abroad the tourist will find his enjoyment increased by a familiarity with the meaning of these symbols, which adorn every specimen of Gothic architecture. It is not necessary that the details of the system shall be fresh in the memory; but a general knowledge of the subject can be easily acquired and retained, and will prove most serviceable.

The preface has acquainted the reader with the reasons for the form of the present treatise. Those who may wish to pursue the subject in full, and to become familiar with the present state of the science, will find the best authorities in the following list : —

Heraldry, Historical and Popular. By the Rev. CHARLES BOUTELL. London: Winsor and Newton. Of this book, three editions have already appeared; the second in 1863, the last in 1864.

The Curiosities of Heraldry, with Illustrations from Old English Writers. By MARK ANTONY LOWER. London: John Russell Smith 1845.

The Pursuivant of Arms; or, Heraldry Founded upon Facts. By J. R. PLANCHÉ, Rouge Croix. London: Robert Hardwicke.

A Glossary of Terms used in British Heraldry, with a Chronological
Table illustrative of its Rise and Progress.   Oxford: John Henry
Parker.   1847.

The Herald and Genealogist.   Edited by JOHN GOUGH NICHOLS,
F.S.A.   London: J. G. Nichols and R. C. Nichols.

This is a magazine of which the first volume appeared in 1863, and
which is now published in six parts annually.   It is especially inter-
esting, as the accomplished editor is now contributing a series of essays
on "The Origin and Development of Coat-Armor."

THE ELEMENTS OF HERALDRY

ELEMENTS OF HERALDRY.

PART I.

§ 1.

IN attempting to give directions for the proper description of coat-armor, which is technically termed the "blazon of arms," it will be convenient to divide such representations into five parts; viz., —

1. The Shield.
2. The Crest.
3. The Supporters.
4. The Helmet and its Mantling, or Lambrequin.
5. The Motto.

1. The shield proper is the object on which the armorial insignia are displayed. It may be of any form, with this exception, — the lozenge or diamond shape is the only form which females can use, and it is reserved for them.

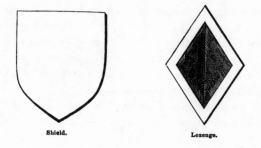

Shield.   Lozenge.

2. The crest is a common adjunct of the shield, and consists of any object or objects placed above it, and used as a hereditary distinction.   It is generally placed upon a wreath or torse made of twisted ribands of the two principal tinctures of the shield; but sometimes the crest surmounts a chapeau, or cap of dignity, in the place of the wreath.   Sometimes, also, the crest rises out of a coronet, the forms of which are hereafter described in the Glossary.

Some of the earliest crests were merely coronets surmounted by feathers : the name for them is " panache." We place below examples of these.

Wreath.   Cap of Dignity.   Panache.

As an illustration of crests, we give the following, showing the wide variety of objects used : —

Crests are not invariably found with shields of arms, and, in fact, are much less distinctive.   Many families use the same crest; and the more common forms are demi-animals, arms bent, and hands holding swords, &c.   The crest is often used alone on seals, and in other ways; but it is especially to be remembered, that *no lady has a right to use a crest:* sovereign princesses are the only exceptions.

3. The supporters which are sometimes placed on each side of the shield, consisting of men or animals, are, in English Her-

aldry, almost the exclusive privilege of peers and members of
certain orders of Knighthood.   A few
families exercise a prescriptive right to
them ; but hardly an instance will probably occur in this country.   They are
more common in Scottish and Continental Heraldry.

An example is here given in the arms
of John, Earl of Bellomont, Governor of
Massachusetts and of New York.

Arms of Earl of Bellomont.

4. The helmet is a well-known object.   Its
use is entirely optional, and it should never be
mentioned in a blazon of arms.   Its place is
between the shield and crest, resting upon the
former.   Many different forms are given, corresponding with the rank of the wearer ; but it
is sufficient to say that it is borne by esquires, in

Helmet.

profile, with the visor closed and turned to the dexter side of the
shield.

The mantling, or lambrequin, is a
small mantle attached to the helmet,
and serving as a background in
paintings of arms.   It is generally
represented as made of crimson vel-
vet, or silk lined with ermine ; and
very often it is cut or torn, giving the
whole an irregular form.   The arrangement is entirely at the discretion
of the artist : often on seals scroll-

Mantling.

work is placed around the shield.   In the above example, we
have the shield placed upon the mantle, and surmounted by the
helmet and wreath, there being no crest shown.

5. The motto, or *cri de guerre*, is a word or sentence upon
a scroll, generally placed below the shield ; but sometimes, especially in Scotland, above it.   It should never be inscribed
upon a garter or circle ; nor should it accompany the arms of
any woman, except the sovereign.   Probably the earliest form

of motto was the rallying cry of the leader; but after coats-of-arms ceased to be used simply in war, a fashion arose of these individual mottoes or sentiments. Generally, they are expressed in Latin. They are not usually confined to a single family, and may be used or varied at the fancy of any individual. Some few, either allusive or historical, are in reality hereditary and distinctive.

§ 2. TINCTURES.

The shield, and all divisions of it, and charges placed thereon, are represented as made of metal or fur, or as painted in colors. These are all included in the general term of "tinctures," and are named and depicted as follows.

First, the two Metals: —

Gold, termed in heraldry *or*, represented in engraving by dots.
Silver, ,,   ,,   ,,   argent, ,,   ,,   ,,   ,, a blank.

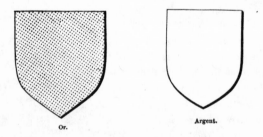

Or.   Argent.

Secondly, the five Colors: —

Blue, termed azure, represented by horizontal lines.
Red,   ,,   gules,   ,,   ,, perpendicular lines.
Black, ,,   sable,   ,,   ,, cross lines.
Green, ,,   vert,   ,,   ,, diagonal lines.
Purple, ,,   purpure, ,,   ,,   ,,   ,,

[NOTE.—Tenné and sanguine, or orange and dark red, are mentioned in treatises on this subject as two additional colors; but they so rarely occur that no description is here given.]

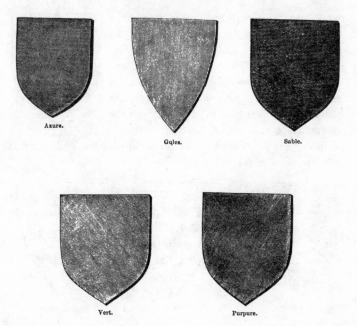

Azure.

Gules.

Sable.

Vert.

Purpure.

The custom is gaining favor, of calling *or* " gold ; " and it is to be commended, inasmuch as this word " or " is not seldom used in blazon in its ordinary sense.

Third, the two Furs and their Variations : —

1. Ermine, which consists of a white field with black spots. The variations are er- mines, being white spots on a black ground ; erminites, differing from ermine by the addi- tion of a red hair on each side the black ; erminois, a golden field with black spots ; pean, a black field with golden spots.

2. Vair, a parti-colored fur of blue and silver (unless other colors are specified), in

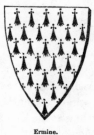

Ermine.

which the pieces are cut in the form of a
shield, and placed in rows alternating the
position in each. Its variation is counter-
vair, in which each row has its shield placed
directly under those of the same color in the
row above; and corresponding to these are
potent and counter-potent, in which the pieces
of fur are crutch-shaped, instead of shield-
shaped. It is believed to be an accidental form of vair: it
consists of a metal and a color.

Vair.

Counter-vair.   Potent.   Counter-potent.

§ 3.   OF THE POINTS OF THE SHIELD.

The shield, for convenience in description, is considered as
having the following points : —

And it is to be remembered, that the shield is considered in its
position to the bearer of it. Thus, the dexter or right-hand
side is to the left of the observer, and the sinister or left-hand side
is on his right.

There are three chief points in the upper part of the shield, three base points at the bottom, and three points in the centre portion, arranged perpendicularly. The arrangement is shown by the above illustration, wherein —

1. is called the dexter chief point.
2. ,, ,, ,, middle chief point.
3. ,, ,, ,, sinister chief point.
4. ,, ,, ,, honor, or collar point.
5. ,, ,, ,, fesse point.
6. ,, ,, ,, nombril, or navel point.
7. ,, ,, ,, dexter base point.
8. ,, ,, ,, middle base point.
9. ,, ,, ,, sinister base point.

§ 4. OF THE DIVISIONS OF THE SHIELD.

The shield may be divided by lines in various ways, and painted of two tinctures. At the same time, certain simple charges placed upon the shield present a similar series of coats; and it seems well to point out the distinction. We may perhaps adopt the following rule : —

The shield is considered as divided whenever the two tinctures occupy equal portions of the field. Whenever one tincture preponderates, it is considered to be the tincture of the shield; and the other tincture is of the charge. There is but one exception; viz., party per chevron; and this will be considered at the end of this section.

Of the divisions, we have simple and compound forms. The simple forms are defined either by one or two lines on the field, and are, —

1. Per pale, made by a perpendicular line.
2. Per fess, made by a horizontal line.
3. Per bend, made by a diagonal line.
4. Per bend sinister, made by a diagonal line.
5. Quarterly, made by the first two lines intersecting.
6. Per saltire, made by the last two lines intersecting.
7. Per chevron, the exception noted above.

Per Pale.   Per Fess.   Per Bend.

Per Bend Sinister.   Quarterly.   Per Saltire.*

Per Chevron.

From a repetition of these forms, but preserving an equal division of the two tinctures of the field, we have the compound forms; viz., —

     8. Paly, a reduplication of per pale.

     9. Barry, a reduplication of per fesse.

     10. Bendy, a reduplication of per bend; and its reverse, from the bend sinister.

---

     * The Flanches seem to be an accidental variation of this division; especially as, in French, party per saltire is termed "flanqué." Still, occupying less than one-half the field, they will be described among the charges.

11. Chequy, or checky, a reduplication of quarterly.

12. Lozengy, a reduplication of per saltire.

13. Gyronny, a compound of quarterly and per saltire; usually consisting of eight pieces, but sometimes of more, formed by more lines, all intersecting at the fess point.

14. Paly-bendy, formed from the pale and bend.

15. Barry-bendy, formed from the bar and bend.

16. Chevronny, formed from the chevron.

Paly.   Barry.   Bendy.

Chequy, or Checky.   Lozengy.   Gyronny.

Paly-bendy.   Barry-bendy.   Chevronny.

The field may be often sprinkled with small figures, previous to receiving the ordinaries or large charges put upon it. These originated in differencing a coat already formed. In early times it was termed "geratty" (*i.e.*, ingerated), but now usually called "semée," as semée of trefoils, cinquefoils, escallops, &c. When semée of crosslets, it was anciently termed "crusilly;" but now the particular form of crosslet is described. Semée of billets is termed "billety;" semée of drops, "guttée;" of fleur-de-lys, "semée-de-lys."

Semee-de-lys.

Guttee.

Crusilly.

Of the exception to the rule, we have to notice that in No. 7, party per chevron, one tincture occupies less than one-half of the shield. Herein English Heraldry differs from French, it being, in the latter, assimilated to the pile. Under the head of "Chevron," we shall consider other peculiarities of this arrangement of lines.

§ 5.   Division Lines.

It is to be noted, that, though these division lines are to be represented as straight, unless otherwise described, they may be of the following forms :—

1. Wavy : 〰〰〰〰
2. Indented : /\/\/\/\/\/\
3. Dancetté : /\/\/\/\, which is a little larger variety of indented.
4. Engrailed : ⌒⌒⌒⌒⌒⌒⌒
5. Invected : ⌣⌣⌣⌣⌣⌣⌣
6. Embattled : ⌐⌐⌐⌐⌐⌐
7. Raguly : ⊿⊿⊿⊿⊿⊿
8. Dovetailed : ⊓⊔⊓⊔⊓⊔⊓
9. Nebuly : ⊃⊂⊃⊂⊃⊂⊃⊂

The same lines are frequently applied to the margin of the principal ordinaries.

§ 6. Charges.

Having considered the shield, its tinctures and divisions, we now proceed to the objects placed thereon, which are termed "charges." The simplest charges correspond in name and position with the divisions of the shield, but are represented as placed upon the shield. It would be useless to speculate upon which form, the division or the charge, first received its name.

These simple charges are termed "ordinaries," and are, —

1. The chief, occupying the upper third of the shield.
2. The fesse,* occupying the centre third horizontally.
3. The pale, occupying the centre third perpendicularly.
4. The bend, occupying one-third of the shield diagonally.
5. The bend sinister,† occupying one-third of the shield diagonally.
6. The cross, being the fesse and pale conjoined, usually occupying one-fifth of the field ; but, when charged, one-third.
7. The saltire, composed of the bend and bend-sinister.
8. The chevron, which resembles the lower half of the saltire, with the upper lines brought to a point.

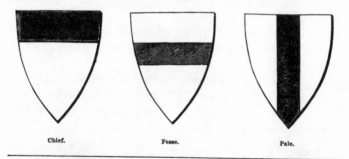

Chief. Fesse. Pale.

---

* It will be noticed that the shield is divided horizontally into three parts, of which the upper and middle sections have names. The lower or base has no specific term ; but, in French, it is termed "la champagne," and its use was revived by Napoleon I. for the arms granted during his reign.

† The bend-sinister is, in French, termed "la barre," and was usually the mark of bastardy. Hence the phrase of "a bar sinister," which has no connection with the English charge of the name. In English Heraldry, illegitimacy is generally denoted by a batôn, or bend-sinister couped at both ends.

Bend.   Bend-sinister.   Cross.

Saltire.   Chevron.

The ordinaries have their diminutives of their own form;
viz., —

1. The chief has the fillet, very probably never used.

2. The pale has the pallet one-half, and the endorse one-
quarter its size. A pale between two endorses is termed "a pale
endorsed."

3. The fesse has no diminutive, unless it be the bar, but is
often put between two bendlets, and is then termed "a fesse
cotised."

4. The bend has the cotise, one-quarter of its size; and, when
between two, it is termed "a bend cotised." However, when
two bends are used, they are of half the usual size, and are
termed "bendlets."

Pale Endorsed.   Fesse Cotised.   Bend Cotised.

5. The chevron has the chevronel, one-half, and the couple-close one-quarter its size. Couple-closes are always borne in pairs : when they are placed on each side of a chevron, it is termed a " chevron cotised."

6. The bar is used as a diminutive of the fesse, probably, and may be placed anywhere except absolutely in chief or in base. Two small bars or barrulets used together are termed "bars gemelles."

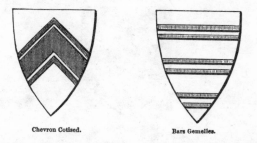

Chevron Cotised.   Bars Gemelles.

Under the head of "Ordinaries" may also be considered the pile, the roundles, and the flanches.

The pile is a wedge-shaped figure, ordinarily issuing from the upper portion of the shield, and occupying one-third of the field. Usually it does not quite touch the edge with its point : it may, however, be drawn from any portion of the shield, and occupy more than one-third.*

Pile.

* In French, however, " la pile " is the charge when pointing towards the base ; and " la pointe " is the charge reversed, and issuing from the base. By a farther distinction in these two cases, the " pile " and the " pointe " occupy only two-thirds of the side from which they spring. When the point occupies the whole, it is termed " chapé ; " and, when the " pile " is of this size, it is termed " chaussé." From the sides, it is termed " embrassé ; " and, lastly, when the " point " occupies only one-quarter, it is termed " mantelé." In all these the idea is, that the smaller tincture is the shield, which is covered over by some wrapper. It will be noticed that " mantelé " is the same as " party per chevron ; " and it would certainly seem well, whenever the terms of heraldry are revised, for our English authorities to adopt the French term, especially as some of the older heralds used the term " a point." The general term " pile " seems to be, on the other hand, a better and simpler designation than the French.

La Pointe Chape.

La Pile Chausse.

Embrasse.

Mantele.

The roundles are circular figures. Formerly, all of these were described by their tinctures, like other charges; but, of late, the fashion is to give them the following names. If of—

Gold, bezants.	Sable, pellets or ogresses.
Argent, plates.	Vert, pommes.
Azure, hurts.	Gules, torteaux.

The fountain is tinctured horizontally with wavy lines, alternately argent and azure.

The flanches are curved figures issuing from each side of the shield, and were probably often accidental variations from per saltire.

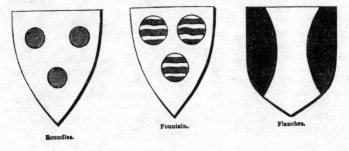

Roundles.　　　　Fountain.　　　　Flanches.

The flasques are doubtless the same; but voiders are very diminutive flanches, never charged, and rarely used.

[NOTE. — We have here to consider one or two simple charges which theoretically ought to occur, but yet do not. Of these the first is the quarter, occupying one-fourth of the shield. Anciently, it was used in the dexter chief; as its diminutive, the canton, still is. Similarly, the other three-fourths of the shield might be used, each as a distinct charge.

Again, as the chevron is used, though very rarely, in all four of the possible divisions of a saltire quartered, we might expect that the cross would be similarly divided, and furnish four charges.

It must be acknowledged, however, that nearly all the writers on heraldry derive the saltire from a leaping-bar, and the chevron from the rafters of a house. NISBET (Heraldry, Edinburgh, 1722) considers the saltire as formed from the bends, and the chevron as derived from the lower portions of the bends, "meeting and ending pyramidically in the collar point." Whoever holds, with us, that the divisions of the shield were based upon a natural system of straight lines, will be satisfied with Nisbet's opinion and authority.]

§ 7. SUB-ORDINARIES.

Under this head may be classed certain charges of frequent occurrence, which are figures peculiar to heraldry. The number of charges to be considered has been varied by almost every writer; but the following list comprises those which have no synonyms in ordinary language : —

1. The canton, a square placed in the dexter chief, and occupying about one-ninth of the shield.

2. The inescutcheon, a small shield borne as a charge. It must not be confounded with the shield of pretence, which is a variety of marshalling. The badge of a baronet is a familiar form of the inescutcheon.

3. The bordure, a border extending around the shield, and one-fifth of its width. It is often charged.

Canton.   Inescutcheon.   Bordure.

4. The orle is an internal bordure, of the form of the shield, but not touching the edge as this latter does.

5. The tressure is a diminutive orle, borne invariably double, fleury-counter-fleury, as in the arms of Scotland.

6. The lozenge, a familiar shape, from which come, —

Orle.

Tressure.

Lozenge.

7. The mascle, a lozenge in outline or skeleton.

8. The rustre, a lozenge with a round aperture in the centre.

9. The fusil, an elongated lozenge.

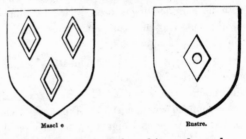

Mascl e.　　　　Rustre.

10. The fret, composed of the saltire and mascle.

11. The billet, a rectangular oblong.

12. The label, a riband with short pendants.

Fret.　　　　Billet.　　　　Label.

13. The annulet, a ring or roundle pierced.

14. The crescent.

15. The fleur-de-lys, a purely heraldic device, which may be derived either from a spear-head or a lily.

Annulet.

Crescent.

Fleur-de-lys.

16. The mullet, or five-pointed star.

17. The estoille or star, heraldic in its shape.

18, 19, 20. The trefoil, quatrefoil, and cinquefoil, composed respectively of three, four, and five leaves, but of a conventional form.

Mullet.

Estoille.

Trefoil.

Quatrefoil.

21. The martlet, a small bird.
22. The escallop or shell.

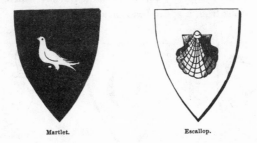

Martlet.   Escallop.

This list embraces, it is believed, all the strictly heraldic figures and divisions usually found. The next chapter will be devoted to an explanation of the terms used by heralds in describing various natural objects used as charges, and representations of the ordinary mode of depicting such objects, as well as their heraldic names. Thus, a lion or a tiger is not to be drawn from a careful study of the actual animal. A certain conventional type has been adopted, which experience proves to be best adapted to give the desired effect to armorial delineations. Much is left to the taste of the artist; but still he is confined within certain bounds.

One remark of the accomplished Planché is worthy of notice : " The number of beasts borne in ancient English coats is not great. In Glover's Roll (temp. Hen. III.), you will find named but three, — the lion, the leopard, and the boar."

In regard to birds, the eagle has the same prominence. Hence the reader will find, that the annexed glossary contains much that will rarely be required. Having carefully studied the names of the tinctures, of the divisions of the shield, and the usual charges, he will require chiefly to learn the distinctive terms employed in describing the position and details of a few well-known charges of frequent occurrence. We may instance the lion, eagle, stag, and various fishes. The mode of distinguishing these particulars will be pointed out in a subsequent chapter on Blazoning Arms.

In the following Glossary, the compiler has chiefly been employed in making extracts from a most valuable Glossary of Heraldry written by Henry Gough, Esq., and published by John Henry Parker, of Oxford, in 1847. In most instances, the definitions of the author have been literally followed, since they were so well expressed that alteration would have been an injury. Still, to secure completeness, the list has been compared with those furnished by other authors, and some few articles re-written in the light of recent investigations and decisions. It is hoped that all the information needed in ordinary cases will be supplied by this list; but the few who desire a thorough knowledge of the subject are referred to the extensive works of Lower, Planché, and Boutell, and to the continued productions of John Gough Nichols, Esq., editor of the "Herald and Genealogist." The antiquary will, of course, turn back to the fanciful books of the past two centuries.

PART II.

A.

A, in heraldic memoranda, is employed to denote argent. In like manner, B is used for blue or azure.

ABASED: a term used when the ordinary is placed lower than its usual position.

ABATEMENTS: these are marks of disgrace placed on the shield of an offender against law. The older treatises are very full of these distinctions; but they are manifestly fanciful, and never actually employed.

ACCOSTED: placed side by side.

ADDORSED, or *Endorsed:* said of two animals placed back to back.

ADUMBRATED: said of a charge depicted with a shadow of the color of the shield. It is rare.

AFFRONTÉ: facing the spectator; or, as applied to two animals facing each other.

ALLERION: an eagle displayed without beak or feet, the point of the wing downward.

ANCIENT: a small flag ending in a point.

ANTELOPE: The conventional type is here given; but it is allowable to represent the animal in its natural form.

Antelope.

APAUMÉ: said of a hand open, showing the palm. This, however, is the ordinary mode of displaying the hand, unless expressly termed "dorsed."

ARCHED : embowed, or bent.

ARM : the human arm is often used as a crest or as a charge. It should be described as "dexter," or "sinister;" also, in regard to position, as "embowed," or "counter-embowed;" and as "naked," "vested," or "vambraced," according to its covering. When couped at the elbow, it is termed a "cubit-arm."

ARMED : whenever any beast of prey has teeth and claws, or any beast of chase (except stags, &c.) has horns and hoof, or any bird of prey has beak and talons, of a tincture different from his body, he is said to be armed of such a tincture. When the term is applied to arrows, it refers to their heads. When a man is said to be *armed at all points*, it signifies that he is entirely covered with armor, except his face.

ARRIÈRE : the back. *Volant en arrière* is the term proper for a bird or insect flying from the spectator upward.

ARRONDIE : made circular or round.

ARROW : the ordinary position of an arrow is in pale with the point downward; but it is well to mention this, — when several arrows are used, the bundle is called a sheaf. Three arrows — two in saltire and one in pale, point downward — are the arms of Lowell. Arrows are *armed* of their point, and *feathered* of the color of their feathers.

AT GAZE : a term applied to stags, &c., represented as standing with the face toward the spectator.

ATTIRE : clothing; also the horns of a stag.

AUGMENTATION : an additional charge granted to a person, by his sovereign, as a special mark of honor.

B.

B, in trickings of arms, means blue or azure.

BADGE, or *Cognizance:* a distinctive emblem adopted by many families; not worn on the helmet like a crest, but used in various modes where a crest is now employed. It was embroidered on the sleeves of servants and followers, and carved or painted in buildings, &c.

BARNACLE: *Horse-barnacle*, or *Pair of Barnacles*, an instrument used by farriers to curb unruly beasts. Usually it is figured as in the cut.

BARON AND FEMME: husband and wife, terms often used in describing impalements.

Barnacle.

BARONET'S BADGE (argent a sinister hand, erect, open, and couped at the wrist gules): This is borne, by all baronets, on a canton, or on an inescutcheon placed on the middle chief-point, or the fess-point, so as least to interfere with the charges on the shield.

BARWISE: horizontally arranged in two or more rows.

BASILISK: see MONSTERS.

Baronet's Badge.

BASNET, or BASINET: a plain circular helmet.

BATON: a diminutive of the bend-sinister, couped at each end. It is the sign of illegitimacy.

BAUDRICK: the sword-belt.

BEAUSEANT: the banner of the Knights Templars. It was an oblong flag, per fesse, sable, and argent, one of the longer sides being fastened to the staff.

Baton.

BEND DEBRUISED, *removed*, or *downset*, a form of this ordinary thus represented. It rarely occurs.

BEZANTÉ: semée of bezants, or gold roundles. Bordures are often so charged, but the present mode is rather to give the number of roundles.

Bend Debruised.

BIRD-BOLT: an arrow with one or more blunt heads, used in shooting birds.

BLEMISHED: a sword with the point broken off is said to be blemished or rebated.

BOLTING: said of a hare or rabbit springing forward.

BRACED : interlaced, as the three chevronels are in the cut.

BREATHING : this word, applied to the stag, is equivalent to *at gaze*.

BUGLE-HORN, or HANCHET : this is generally painted with its cords, and with the larger end towards the dexter side.

Chevronels Braced.

C.

CABOSSED : applied to the head of any beast except a leopard, when borne full faced, no part of the neck being visible.

CALTRAP : an iron instrument made with spikes, placed on the ground, so that one was always erect.

Bugle-horn.

CAREERING : a term applied to a horse in a position which would be called salient if a beast of prey were spoken of.

CARTOUCHE : an oval escutcheon used by popes and other Italian ecclesiastics.

CASQUE : a helmet.

CASTLE : usually a tower alone, or two towers with a gate between them.

Cabossed.

CHAPLET : a garland of leaves with four flowers amongst them at equal distances.

CHESS-ROOK : a common bearing, often confounded with a castle.

CLOUÉ : nailed.

COCKATRICE : see MONSTERS.

COLLEGE OF ARMS :* the English College of Arms was in-

* In Scotland the Lyon Office, and in Ireland the Office of arms occupy the same position as the College of Arms. Each has one King of Arms, Lord Lyon and Ulster. The English College of Arms has for its head the Earl Marshal of England, an office held by the Duke of Norfolk, and hereditary in his family. Anciently, the Earl Marshal had the power to compel all persons falsely assuming arms to renounce and remove such arms. For the purpose of recording the true coats-of-arms, visitations were made every few years to the different

corporated by King Richard III. in 1483. In 1622 the officers, whose number. and titles had varied from time to time, were fixed as follows : —

Kings-at-arms, Garter, Clarenceux, Norroy.

Heralds, Lancaster, Somerset, Richmond, Windsor, York, Chester.

Pursuivants, Rouge-Croix, Blue-Mantle, Portcullis, Rouge-Dragon.

COMBATANT : said of two lions rampant face to face.

CONTOURNÉ : turned to the sinister.

COMET, or BLAZING-STAR : an estoile of six points with a tail extending from it in bend.

COMPARTMENT : a term peculiar to Scottish Heraldry, being a panel placed below the shield. It usually bears the motto, and the supporters stand upon it.

COMPONÉ, or GOBONÉ : said of an ordinary, composed of small squares of two tinctures alternately in one row. If there be two rows, it is called "counter-compony ; " if three, "checquy."

CONFRONTÉ : said of two animals facing each other.

CONJOINED : joined together.

COOTE : a water-fowl so called.

CORBIE : a raven.

CORDED : bound with cords.

CORDON, or CORDILIÈRE : a silver cord which sometimes encircles the arms of widows.

CORNISH CHOUGH : a bird with a black body and red beak and legs.

CORONET : different forms are used in England to denote the

counties; and the gentry were invited to have their claims verified and recorded. The lists then made, technically termed "visitations," are preserved at the College, and constitute the highest authority for the use of arms. This power of the Earl Marshal has fallen into disuse; though in Scotland the authority of the Lord Lyon, King of Arms, is still invoked to prevent any flagrant and conspicuous breach of his laws.

"The present duty of Heralds," according to Boutell, "comprises Grants of Arms; the Tracing and Drawing-up of Genealogies; the Recording Arms and Genealogies in the registers of the Heralds' College; recording the Creation and Succession of Peers and others, with all similar matters, including the Direction of Royal Pageants and Ceremonials."

rank of the wearer. A crest often rises out of what is improperly termed a "ducal coronet." The modern term for it is a "crest coronet."

Chevron Couched.

COUCHANT : said of beasts lying down, but with the head erect.

COUCHED : a chevron issuing from the side is said to be couched.

COUNTER-CHANGED : applied to charges upon a field composed of a color and a metal in a primary division. The charges on each side of the division line are of the tincture of the field on the other side.

COUNTER-COUCHANT : the precise meaning of this term depends upon the rest of the description. Thus : two lions accosted counter-couchant means that they lie side by side, with their heads in contrary directions. Again : two lions counter-couchant in pale denotes that one occupies the upper part of the shield and the other the lower ; one facing the dexter, the other the sinister. One lion counter-couchant always faces the sinister.

COUPED : cut off in a straight line, a term especially used in regard to heads and limbs of animals. Ordinaries are sometimes said to be couped, but more often they are termed "humetté."

COURANT : running a full speed.

COUSU : sewed to. Sometimes a chief or canton is of the same denomination as the field ; and this term is used to avoid the rule, that color shall not be placed on color, or metal on metal.

COWARD, *Cowed* or *Coué :* said of a beast having his tail hanging between his legs, and usually bent over his back.

CRAMP, or CRAMPOON : a piece of iron bent at each end ; they are generally borne in pairs.

Crampoon.

CRAMPET, *Chape*, or *Boteroll :* the metal termination of a scabbard.

CRENELLÉ : the same as embattled. See DIVISION LINES.

CRESCENT : a half-moon, with the horns uppermost. When the horns are turned to the dexter side of the shield, it is an "Increscent ;" when turned to the sinister, a "Decrescent."

CREVICE : the écrevisse, or crawfish.

CRINED : said of the hair or mane when of a different tincture from the body of the man or animal.

CROSS : the plainest form has been already given as an ordinary. This form, with many of the following, may be drawn with all the lines of division, as engrailed, raguly, &c. ; and also couped, voided, parted, &c.

The following list comprises the forms commonly used in English Heraldry : —

CROSS AVELLANE : so called from its resemblance to filberts (*nuces avellanæ*).

CROSS-CROSSLET : with each composed of a cross. (It is often fitché or sharpened at the bottom.)

Cross Avellane.   Cross-crosslet.   Cross-crosslet crossed.

CROSS-CROSSLET CROSSED, or four cross-crosslets conjoined.

CROSS CROSSED : like the cross-crosslet, with the ends extended to the side of the shield.

CROSS DEGRADED and CONJOINED : a plain cross, having its extremities placed upon steps joined to the sides of the shield.

CROSS PATÉE, or FORMÉE : with curved sides and straight ends.

CROSS POTENT : terminating in potents or crutches. In this example, it is *between* four crosslets.

Cross degraded and conjoined.   Cross patée, or formée.   Cross potent.

CROSS BOURDONÉE, or POMEL: terminating in four round knots.

CROSS BOTTONNÉE: with a triple button at each end.

CROSS POINTED, or URDÉE: with the ends pointed and sides straight.

Cross bourdonnée, or pomel.

Cross bottonnée.

Cross pointed, or urdée.

CROSS CLECHÉE: similar, but with curved sides.

CROSS MOLINE: with ends formed of two curved leaves.

CROSS PATONCE: terminating in three leaves.

CROSS FLEURY: differing from the patonce, as the sides are straight.

Cross Moline.

Cross Patonce.

Cross Fleury.

CROSS FOURCHÉE, and

CROSS MILLER: variations of the cross moline, probably.

CROSS MALTESE: or of eight points.

Cross Fourchée.

Cross Miller.

Cross Maltese.

CROSS OF FOUR ERMINE SPOTS.

CROSS TAU, or OF ST. ANTHONY.

CROSS PATRIARCHAL : with two horizontal bars.

Cross of four ermine spots.   Cross Tau.   Cross Patriarchal.

CROSS CALVARY : a plain cross raised upon three steps.

CROSS VOIDED : when the outline only is left, the cross is said to be "voided."

CROSS RAGULY : with sides regularly notched.

Cross Calvary.   Cross voided.   Cross raguly.

CROWN : generally in blazon. This means a ducal coronet without the cap, and showing only three leaves. An animal crowned is always so depicted, unless otherwise stipulated.

CUP : there are several kinds of cups used in heraldry. The usual form is a plain open cup; but the Butlers bear a covered cup.

CUSHIONS : usually represented as a square, with tassels at each corner.

D.

DEBRUISED : ordinarily said of an animal having a charge placed over it, and over part of the field.

DECRESCENT : a half-moon whose horns are turned to the sinister, — the reverse of increscent.

DEGRADED : placed upon steps, as in the case of a cross.

DEMI : half. When said of animals, the upper part is always meant ; when of inanimate objects, usually the dexter part per pale.

DIAPER : a term applied to the field of shields and charges when decorated with damask or arabesque work not intended to be part of the tincture. A familiar example would be arms painted on metal, but chased also with a graver. BOUTON gives some beautiful examples, and recommends a revival of the fashion, as a highly ornamental adjunct to the use of coat-armor in decoration.

Eagle displayed.

DIMIDIATION: a division in halves. Shields were thus literally joined before the mode of impaling was adopted.

DISCLOSED : said of a bird with the wings open, but pointing downward.

DISPLAYED : expanded. Used chiefly in reference to the eagle, which is commonly thus represented.

DOLPHIN : a well-known fish, usually represented as embowed or bent.

DRAGON : see MONSTERS.

Dolphin Embowed.

E.

EEL-SPEAR : a fork used for taking eels.

EMBOWED : bent, as the arm at the elbow. Hence we have bowed counter embowed, said of two objects bent in opposite ways and facing each other; and bowed embowed, or doubly bent like a letter S.

Embowed.

EMBRUED : objects bloody or with drops of blood falling from them are termed "embrued."

EMERASSES, or AILETTES : small escutcheons affixed to the shoulders of an armed knight.

ENFILED : a sword is said to be enfiled with any object which it is represented as having pierced.

ENHANCED : said of a chevron or other ordinary borne higher than its usual place.

ENSIGNED : a shield surmounted by a crown, coronet, or mitre, is said to be ensigned with it.

ERADICATED : said of a tree torn up by the roots.

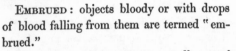

Erased.

ERASED : having a torn edge. Applied chiefly to the heads and limbs of animals.

ESCARBUNCLE, ESCARBONCLE, or CAR-BUNCLE : a peculiarly heraldic device.— Though sometimes said to represent the gem carbuncle, Planché has rendered it evident that it is derived from the centre boss placed at the interlacing point of transverse bars used to strengthen the shield.

Escarbuncle, Escarboncle, or
Carbuncle.

F.

FEMME : used heraldically for wife, as baron is for husband.

FER-DE-MOULINE, or MILL-RIND : said to be the iron which upholds a mill-stone. The essential point of it seems to be, that it shall be a saltire, pierced in the centre ; but the forms are innumerable.

FESSE-WISE : said of objects borne horizontally in the middle of the field.

FETTERLOCK : a form of lock similar to a handcuff or letter D, in which the curved

Fer-de-mouline, or Mill-rind.

part is hinged on one end of the straight part, and fastens at the other end.

FIMBRIATED : said of a charge having a narrow edging of another tincture all round it. Herein it is held to differ from *edged*, a term used when the edging is only on the part towards the field.

FISH : when not otherwise specified, a conventional form is used.

FLEXED : the same as embowed.

FRACTED : broken.

FRAZIER, or FRAZE : in French, a strawberry plant, — probably always represented by a cinquefoil.

FRUCTED : bearing fruit.

FUMANT : emitting smoke.

Fusilly.

FUSILLY : charges formed with fusils are thus termed.

FYLFOT, or GAMMADION : a charge of unknown origin. It has been termed " the mark of Thor's hammer," and it has also been proved to be a sacred emblem in India. It is very rarely used as a charge.

Fylfot, or Gammadion.

G.

Garbe.

GARBE : a wheat sheaf; when of any other grain, it must be specified, as a " garbe of oats." When the stalks are of one tincture and the ears of another, the term *eared* is used of the latter.

GARDANT : said of an animal with the face turned toward the spectator. See LION.

GARNISHED : ornamented.

GAUNTLET : a mailed glove, respectively termed " sinister " and " dexter."

Gore.

GED : a fish also known as the lucy, or pike.

GENET : an animal resembling a fox, but smaller ; and usually depicted as gray, spotted with black.

GERATTY : an old term for semée.

GORE : a charge formed of two curved lines. It may be on either side of the shield.

GORGED : collared. When used alone, a plain collar is meant ; but animals are often gorged with a coronet.

Gurges.

GRAY : a badger.

GRICE : a young wild boar.

GRIFFIN : see MONSTERS.

GURGES : a whirlpool; figured as in the margin.

GUSSET : a charge, probably fanciful, formed of two straight lines. It may be on either side, or two may be used in a pair.

Gusset.

H.

HABITED : clothed.

HAMMERS are of various shapes.

HAURIENT : breathing; a term applied to a fish in an erect position.

HAWK'S BELL : a little circular bell used on hawks.

HAWK'S LURE : a decoy used in falconry.

HEAD : the human head occurs on many shields and crests, and the kind intended should be specified in the blazon.

HEART : the human heart is represented in the ordinary conventional mode.

HEIGHTENED : see ENHANCED.

HERRISON : the French term for hedgehog.

HIRONDELLE : the swallow.

HUMETTY : couped; said of ordinaries only.

HYDRA : see MONSTERS.

Hawk's lure.

I.

IBEX : probably the same as the antelope in tricking arms.

INCENSED : said of wild beasts represented with fire issuing from their mouths and ears.

INCRESCENT : a half moon with the horns turned to the dexter side of the shield.

ISSUANT : said of a charge rising from the bottom line of a field or chief, or the upper line of a fesse, or from a coronet. It differs from "Naissant," which see.

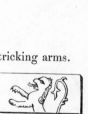

Issuant.

J.

JAMBE, or GAMBE: the leg of a beast. If couped or erased at the middle joint, it is a paw.

JELLOPED: said of the comb and gills of a cock or cockatrice, when of a different tincture from his body.

JESSANT: springing forth. Probably this is used chiefly in the phrase following.

Jambe, or Gambe.

JESSANT-DE-LYS: said of a leopard's head, pierced by fleur-de-lys.

JESSES: thongs, by which bells are fastened to the legs of falcons.

K.

KNOTS of various kinds are used, some with specific names, as Harrington's, Stafford's, Lacy's, &c.

Jessant-de-lys.

L.

LAMB: Holy or Paschal; represented with a nimbus round the head, and as bearing a flag.

LANGUED: said of animals having the tongue of a color different from the body. Usually, it is proper, or gules.

LATTISED: a pattern similar to fretty, but placed crossways. It is often cloué, or shown as nailed at each crossing. It is also termed "Treillé."

Holy Lamb.

Leopard : always borne gardant or full-faced, as opposed to the lion usually borne with the face in profile. Modern heraldry has abolished this distinction, and represents the leopard with his spots. A leopard's head should show the neck erased; and a leopard's face, the head turned to the spectator, without the neck.

Leopard's head.

Letters of the alphabet occur in some shields.

Lever : the cormorant.

Lily, or Lys of the Field : the usual style of lily.

Lion : usually depicted in the heraldic style, with tufts of hair on his body, &c. The usual forms of the charge are, —

1. Rampant.
2. Passant.
3. Gardant.

Rampant.

Passant.

Gardant.

4. Rampant-regardant.
5. Passant-gardant.
6. Passant-regardant.

Rampant-regardant.

Passant-gardant.

Passant-regardant.

7. Couchant.
8. Coward.
9. Sejant rampant.

Couchant.   Coward.   Sejant rampant.

10. Statant.
11. Salient.

Statant.   Salient.

Lions may be also conjoined, or bicorporated, or incorporated; but these are probably rare forms.

A Demi-lion shows the tail; differing, thus, from a lion's head couped.

Demi-lion.

He may also be Dismembered, or Dechaussé, when divided by cuts, but the portions left in place so as to show the outline.

Lions are often represented with two tails, or "queue fourchée."

LIONCELS: several lions in one coat are sometimes thus termed; but the distinction is perhaps fanciful.

LIZARD, or LEZARD: an animal resembling a wildcat, with brown fur, and spots of a darker shade.

Dechaussé.

The reptile lizard also occurs, and is properly vert.

LODGED : couchant; especially applied to stags, &c.

LUCY : a fish now known as the pike.

LURE : two wings joined with their tips downward are said to be *conjoined in* lure. The reference is to the *hawk's lure*, already explained.

LUTRA, LOUTRE, or LOUTEREL : the otter.

LYMPHAD, or GALLEY : an ancient ship with one mast, and rowed with oars, which are usually represented.

Lodged.

M.

MAJESTY, IN HIS : said of an eagle crowned and holding a sceptre. The idea is like that of a pelican in its piety, or a peacock in his pride.

MARCASSIN : a young wild boar; distinguished from an old one by having his tail hanging down instead of twisted.

MARTEL : a kind of hammer.

MASONED : said of a field or charge divided by lines resembling masonry.

MATCH : a coil anciently used for the purpose of discharging firearms.

MAUNCH, or MANCH : an ancient sleeve, used quite often in coats-of-arms; two forms are here given.

Maunch, or Manch.

Maunch, or Manch.

MEMBRED : said of the legs of birds when of a different tincture from the body.

MERCHANTS' MARKS. Very often wealthy merchants, not entitled to arms, bore on a shield a device. Often this device consisted of a figure resembling the numeral 4, turned back, with the addition of initials variously arranged. Seals made in this style are very often found.

MERMAID : see MONSTERS.

MORION : a steel cap worn by foot-sol-diers.

MORSE : a term for a sea-lion.

MOUND ROYAL : an orb surmounted by a cross, usually pattée.

MOUNTING : rampant.

MUSION : an old heraldic term for a cat.

Mound Royal.

MONSTERS : Lower's "Curiosities of Heraldry," p. 91, gives the following list of heraldic monsters : —

Allerion.	Montegre.
Chimera.	Opinicus.
Cockatrice.	Pegasus.
Dragon.	Sagittary.
Griffin.	Satyr.
Harpy.	Sphinx.
Lion-Dragon.	Unicorn.
Lion-Poisson.	Winged Bull.
Martlet.	Winged Lion.
Mermaid.	Wyvern.

Of these, the Allerion and Martlet are elsewhere described.

The Sagittary is the Centaur of antiquity, half man and half horse. The Mermaid and the Unicorn are too well known to require description. The Chimera, Harpy, Sphinx, and Satyr are also of the antique type. The Montegre, or Man-tyger, had the body of a tiger, the head of an old man, and the horns of an ox. The monsters peculiarly heraldic, there-fore, seem to be the —

Cockatrice.
Dragon.
Griffin.
Wyvern.

Cockatrice.

Dragon.

Griffin.

Wyvern.

Which are best understood by the engraved examples. The Opinicus is very similar to the Griffin, but has four legs and a short tail.

N.

NAIANT: swimming horizontally.

NAISSANT: said of a charge springing from the *middle* of an ordinary. Herein it differs from "Issuant."

NOWED: twisted, or knotted.

NOWY implies a round projection in the middle of a cross or other ordinary. It may however be nowy-lozengy, nowy-masculy, or nowy-quadrate, as it is lozenge, or mascle-shaped, or square.

Naissant.

O.

OPINICUS : see MONSTERS.

OVER ALL, or SURTOUT : said of a charge placed over several other charges.

OVERT : open ; applied to the wings of birds.

OWLS are always depicted as full-faced.

P.

PALL : a figure of the shape of the upper half of a saltire, joined to the lower half of a pale, or of the letter Y. It is commonly held to represent an ecclesiastical vestment ; but French authors hold it to be simply a combination of the halves of the bend, bend sinister, and pale.

PASCUANT, or PAISSANT : feeding ; applied only to cattle and sheep.

PATTÉE : spreading.

PAW : see JAMBE.

PEA-RISE : a pea-stalk with flowers and leaves.

PEEL : a baker's shovel.

Pelican.

PELICAN : a bird always represented with wings endorsed, and as *vulning* or wounding herself. When feeding her young in the nest, she is termed *in her piety*.

PHEON : a spear-head ; the point is always downward, unless otherwise described.

PHŒNIX : see MONSTERS.

PIERCED : said of any charge which is perforated so that the field is there seen.

Pheon.

Also it is said of a charge passing through another, as a chevron pierced with a bend.

Pierced.

PINE-APPLE : by this term the pine cone was meant; but in modern times the true fruit has been sometimes depicted where the blazon meant the cone.

PLANTA GENISTA : the broom-plant; well known as the badge of the Plantagenet Kings of England.

POMETTY : said of a cross or escarbuncle having a circular projection in the middle of each arm.

POPINJAY : a parrot, depicted as vert, beaked and membered gules.

PORTCULLIS : a frame of wood, strengthened and spiked with iron, used for the defence of the gate of a castle.

POSED : placed.

POTENT : the old name for a crutch; whence the name of a cross ending in this shape, and also that. of the fur described in our first part.

POUNCING : said of a falcon seizing his prey.

PPR : the abbreviation of proper; the term for objects represented of their common form and color.

PREYING UPON : devouring.

PRIDE, IN HIS : said of a peacock affronté, with his tail expanded.

PRIMROSE : a term sometimes applied to the quatrefoil.

PURFLED : ornamented.

PYOT : a magpie.

Q.

QUADRATE : square.

QUADRATURE, IN, means that four charges are placed at the corners of an imaginary square.

QUARTERLY QUARTERED: said of a saltire thus divided.

QUEUED: tailed. A lion with two tails
is said to be double-queued.

QUILLED: said of the porcupine, or of a
feather in which the quill is of a different
tincture from the rest.

QUISE, or CUISSE, A LA: said of the leg
of a bird torn off at the thigh.

Quarterly quartered.

R.

RADIANT, or RAYONNÉ: edged with rays.

RAGULY: said of an ordinary, having pieces couped project-
ing from it in a slanting direction. An instance will be seen in
the Cross Raguly.

RAVEN: the bird usually so called. It is also called in heraldry a Corbie.

REBATED: having the points cut off.

REGARDANT: said of animals having the head turned back.

REINDEER: distinguished from the stag by double attires,
one pair erect, the other pendent.

REMOVED signifies that an ordinary has fallen from its usual
place. The reversed of Enhanced.

RENVERSÉ: said of any thing with its head placed opposite
to the usual way.

RERE-MOUSE: the bat; always borne displayed.

REST, SUFFLUE, or CLARION: a heraldic
figure of unknown origin.

REVERSED: turned upside down.

RISING: preparing for flight; said of a
bird with wings opened.

ROMPU: broken.

ROOK: the bird so called; sometimes
improperly used for a Chess-Rook.

Rest, Sufflue, or Clarion.

ROSE : this flower should never be drawn with a stalk, unless so described.   The color should also be specified.

S.

SACRE, or SAKER : a species of falcon.   Its head is gray, the back dark-brown, and the legs light-blue.

SAGGITARY : see MONSTERS.

SALIENT : said of a beast represented as springing on its prey.   Counter-salient is said of two leaping in different ways, that facing the dexter being generally above the other.

SANGLANT : bloody, embrued.

SANGLIER : a wild boar.

SANS : without.

SCRIP, PILGRIM'S : a pouch, or wallet.

SEA-MEW : the sea-gull, or curlew.

SEA-PYE : a maritime bird of a dark-brown color, with a white breast.

SEAX : a broad, curved sword, with a semicircular notch on the back of the blade.

SEEDED : shown its seeds, as in a rose.

SEGREANT : having the wings expanded; applied to the Griffin.

SEJANT, or ASSIS : seated.   See an example under " Lion."

SHACK-BOLT : a manacle, or handcuff.

SHELDRAKE : a sea-fowl nearly resembling a duck.

SHOVELLER : a species of duck; distinguished by two small tufts of feathers, one at the back of the head, the other on the breast.

SKEEN, or SKENE : a dagger.

SLIPPED : having a stalk; used in describing trefoils and flowers.

SOLEIL : the sun; used especially in the phrase, "a rose en soleil," or "a rose surrounded with rays."

SPRINGING : beasts of chase in the position in which wild beasts are called salient are said to be springing.

STATANT: standing with all the feet touching the ground. A stag, however, in this position, is called "at gaze."

SUN: the sun is usually borne *in his glory* or *splendor*, *i.e.*, with a human face, and rays alternately straight and wavy.

SURMOUNTED: said of a charge placed over another of a different tincture, and preserving its form.

SYKES: fountains.

T.

TALBOT: a hunting-dog; distinguished by the form of his ears.

TARGE, or TARGET: a shield.

TERGIANT: having the back turned to the spectator.

THROUGHOUT: extending to the sides of the shield.

TIERCÉE: divided into three equal parts; said of a shield.

Talbot.

TIMBER, or TYMBRE: a crest.

TOISON: the fleece of a sheep.

TORQUED: wreathed.

TREFLÉE: adorned with Trefoils.

TRIPPANT: equivalent to passant, and applied to beasts of chase.

TRIVET: a frame of iron with three feet.

TRUNCATED, or TRUNKED: couped.

TRUSSED: said of birds otherwise termed "close."

TYGER: the heraldic tiger is thus depicted.

TYRWHITT: the lapwing.

Tiger.

U.

UNGULED : having hoofs.

UNICORN : see MONSTERS.

URINANT : diving ; said of fish with the head downwards.

V.

VAMBRACED : said of an arm covered with armor.

VOIDED : having the middle removed so that the shield is seen between the two parts.

VOLANT : flying bend-ways towards the dexter.

VORANT : devouring.

VULNED : wounded and bleeding. When the weapon (as an arrow) remains in the wound, the animal is said to be transfixed.

W.

WATER-BOUGET : a yoke with two leather pouches appended, used to carry water. There are many forms.

WATTLED : said of the gills of the cock and cockatrice.

WHEEL : usually of eight spokes. The Katherine-wheel is armed with teeth.

WOLF : the animal is thus figured.

WREATHED : said of ordinaries represented as twisted, or formed like a rope.

WYVERN : see MONSTERS.

Katherine-wheel.

Wolf.

PART III.

¶ 1.

ON THE BLAZON OF ARMS.

By the term "blazon" is meant "the verbal description of a coat-of-arms, so precise as to enable the reader to depict the escutcheon correctly, without other assistance."

The rules universally adopted in such descriptions of arms are as follows : —

1. The field is first to be described, whether of one tincture or two. If of two, the form of division is to be mentioned, as per pale, per fesse, or barry, &c. ; and also the division-line as engrailed, wavy, &c.

2. If semée, with small charges, these must be mentioned ; as also if the field be fretty.

3. The principal ordinary (except the chief) is next to be named. If there be none, the principal charge, being the one nearest the fesse-point, or centre of the shield ; and this must be fully described, *i.e.*, all peculiarities of form, tincture, or position.

4. The remaining charges placed on the field are to be described ; the centre charge being described as "between," or "surrounded by," or "within" them. Their place must also be described, unless there are three placed, two in chief and one in base, which is regarded as the usual mode. Six of a kind are arranged, unless otherwise mentioned, three, two,

and one. In the same way, a greater number, as ten or fifteen, are so placed as to preserve the pyramidical shape. When a bend is between six charges of a kind, the upper three are placed two and one, and the lower three in a line following the curve of the shield.

5. Next, the charges on the principal charge are to be given.

6. The bordure with the charges thereon are to be mentioned.

7. The canton, or chief, with all charges thereon, are to be given.

8. Lastly, the differences, or marks of cadency, and the baronet's badge, are enumerated.

The crest, supporters, and motto are to be separately blazoned after the shield.

In blazon, repetition should be avoided: the name of a tincture should not be repeated, but instead should be used the phrase, "of the first," "second," or "third," &c., as the case may be; the numeral referring to the place of the tincture in the blazon.

When two or more consecutive portions of the blazon are of the same tincture, it may be mentioned only after the last. Thus, a chevron gules between three crescents gules would be blazoned, "a chevron between three crescents gules." So also when the number of objects in different parts of the blazon is the same, the phrase "as many" is to be employed; for example, a chevron between three crescents, and in chief three crosses, would be rendered "a chevron between three crescents, and in chief *as many* crosses."

The learner need not be discouraged, should his description at first be too diffuse. So long as he can describe all the portions of the coat, giving such particulars as will enable another to depict it perfectly, he may be sure that he has acquired the essential part of the science.

As examples of the mode of blazon, we give the following:—

Wheelwright.

Steel.

Priuce.

Thatcher.

1. Wheelwright: Ermine, on a fesse gold between three wolf's heads erased (sable?), as many roundles gules. Crest, a wolf's head erased. [It will be noticed that the tincture of the wolf's heads is not marked by the engraver.]

2. Steel: Argent, a bend counter-compony, ermine, and (sable) between two lion's heads erased (gules); on a chief (azure), three billets (of the third). Crest, a lion's head erased (gules).

3. Prince: Gules, a saltire gold, surmounted of a cross engrailed ermine. Crest: out of a ducal coronet gold, a cubit arm, habited gules, cuffed ermine, holding in the hand proper three pine-apples of the first, stalked and leaved vert.

4. Thatcher: Gules, a cross moline argent; on a chief gold, three grasshoppers proper. Crest, a sword erect, point downwards.

It has already been said, that it is a cardinal rule in English heraldry, that metal must not be placed on metal, nor color

upon color, though either of them can be used over or under
fur. This sweeping rule requires, no doubt, some modification.
Thus it cannot apply to charges placed "over all;" as, for
example, in the following coat, "argent a cross gules, over all
a bend azure." So also where the field is of two tinctures, a
metal and a color, the charge must, in most cases, be one
or the other; as "barry of twelve gold and azure, an eagle
displayed gules."

The rule is not so strict in Continental heraldry; but in
English the only cases in which a simple charge is placed on
a plain shield of the same class of tincture are the few in
which it is done for the purpose of attracting attention. Thus
the arms of the Kingdom of Jerusalem, established by the Cru-
saders, were, "argent, a cross potent between four plain crosses
gold."

¶ 2.

ON MARSHALLING ARMS.

The foregoing rules apply to each shield considered by itself;
but we frequently find two or more coats arranged together
upon a large shield. When two coats are placed thus side by
side, they are always intended to represent the coats of a husband and wife; the former occupying the dexter, the latter the
sinister, half of the shield. This is termed "impaling." As
an example, we give the arms of Bulkley impaling Chetwode.

Here we have Bulkley, "argent, a
chevron between three bull's heads
cabossed, sable," impaling Chetwode
"quarterly, argent and gules, four crosses pattée counterchanged."

Bulkley.

Every *armiger* has the right thus to
use his wife's family arms, even after
her death: in case of a second marriage, however, it is customary to cease

the use of the first wife's arms. A wife, or a widow while
remaining such, has the right to use the impaled coat, but in a
lozenge.

A maid bears her paternal coat in a lozenge.

Impaling, as we have said, is of universal application; but a
different mode is used in one particular case. If the wife be
an heiress, *heraldically* (*i.e.*, if she had no brother, or he
be deceased childless), the husband, instead of impaling her
arms, places them upon a small shield covering the centre point
of his own shield, which is termed an " escutcheon of pretence."

An example will be found in the arms of the Earl of Bellomont (*ante*, p. 3), who thus bore the arms of his wife, Cath-
erine, daughter and heir of —— Nanfan, of Bridgemorton,
county of Worcester.

It is to be noted, that though the different sons ought to use
some mark of cadency, as hereafter explained, (see p. 62) the
daughters do not; but are considered as equally heiresses, and
their husbands have all an equal right to bear the arms on an
escutcheon of pretence.

The other mode in which two coats are combined on one
shield is termed " quartering."   Ordinarily, an *armiger* has
no right to use his mother's arms; that is, in case she had a
brother to continue the family name, the arms descending exclusively in the male line of the posterity of the original recipient,
so long as it continues.   The children of an heiress, however,
inasmuch as they become the representatives in blood of the last
owner of the arms in their branch, have a right to use their
mother's arms in a certain mode.

This method is termed " quartering; " and
the arms of the mother are placed in the second
and third quarters of a shield, the first and
fourth being occupied by the paternal arms.
In the following example, we have Moseley
quartering another coat; viz., first and fourth,
Moseley, "sable, a chevron between three mill-
picks argent: " second and third, gold a fesse
(—?) between three eagles displayed sable.

Moseley.

This is the simplest form of quartering, and refers to one marriage only. It will be readily seen, that an *armiger* thus entitled to a quartered coat might marry an heiress, and his children would have another coat to add to their shield. In this case, it is usual to place the paternal coat in the first and fourth quarters, and the two coats acquired by marriage in the second and third respectively.

Our illustration represents a quartered coat impaling a simple coat; being Pownall quartering Browne, and impaling Churchill.

It will be perceived, that there is hardly any limit to the number of coats which may thus be inherited by an *armiger*. As an heiress inherits a

Pownall, &c.

quartered coat and transmits it to her children, by a series of such marriages an immense number of shields are brought together for arrangement. In this case, the shield is divided into the requisite number of spaces by horizontal and perpendicular lines, and in the first quarter are placed the paternal arms, next the arms acquired by the earliest match, and so on; observing that the divisions are numbered from the first quarter, towards the sinister on the chief, and so downward in successive rows, counting from the dexter side.

When many quarterings belong to an *armiger*, the whole are only used for special purposes; but any of them may be selected for use. He has probably no right to drop his own arms, and use one of the quarterings alone, as there are generally many other heirs equally entitled to use them.

As an example of impalements, we will take the arms of Samuel Appleton, who emigrated from Little Waldingfield, county of Suffolk, to New England in 1635, and was the progenitor of a well-known family here.

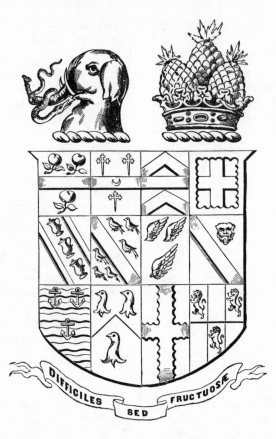

This shield contains twelve quarterings, or separate coats-of-arms. As before stated, the first shield occupies the dexter chief, and is that of Appleton. Argent, a fesse sable between three apples gules, leaves and stalk vert. The full list is as follows :—

1. Appleton.	5. Boteler.	9. Condy.
2. Crane.	6. Mountney.	10. Tuke.
3. Mollington.	7. Sexton.	11. Hawte.
4. Carbonel.	8. Isaack.	12. Wheathill.

We will next explain the cause of the order in which they appear.   The pedigree stands thus : —

Thomas Apulton ═ Margaret, dau. and heir of Robert Crane (No. 2).

Robert Appilton ═ Mary, dau. and heir of Thomas Mountney (No. 6).

William A. ═ Rose, dau. and heir of Robert Sexton (No. 7).

Thomas ═ Mary, dau. and heir of Edward Isaack (No. 8).

Samuel A. ═ Mary Everard.
4th son.

We here see that the first marriage with Crane brought one quartering, No. 2 : but she was entitled to quarter Nos. 3, 4, and 5 ; and these, therefore, follow her own paternal coat. Then we have Nos. 6, 7, and 8, brought in by successive marriages : but the Isaacs, No. 8, had the right to quarter four other coats, which are here represented consecutively as Nos. 9, 10, 11, and 12.

It will be noticed that it is usual to make the shield in such form as to contain just the number of impalements ; but, if necessary, the first coat may be repeated for the last.   Thus, in this example, had it happened that there were but eleven coats to quarter, the shield might have been narrowed so as to afford room for but three coats in the base, or lower row, or the Appleton coat might have been repeated as the twelfth coat.

[NOTE. — Though we do not find it expressly stated, it is probable that crests do not pass with the coats that are quartered. The reason would seem to be, that, as no female can use a crest, she does not inherit one, and consequently her children are debarred from such use.]

¶ 3.

CADENCY.

Lastly, we have to consider what are termed " the marks of cadency," being certain additions to the shield to denote the genealogical status of the bearer of a coat.

The heralds of the seventeenth century, a period when the science was at its lowest point, adopted the following scheme. The sons of an *armiger* were to use the paternal arms, but to place in chief the following charges : —

The first son, a label; the second, a crescent; the third, a mullet; the fourth, a martlet; the fifth, an annulet; the sixth, a fleur-de-lys; the seventh, a rose; the eighth, a cross moline; the ninth, a double quatrefoil.

In the next generation, the badge was to be charged with a new one for each son, in the same order. Thus the sixth son of the second son would have a crescent charged with a fleur-de-lys. This system was to be continued *ad infinitum*, but it was too preposterous. It still holds its place nominally in text-books, but is probably never used.

Boutell, however, has pointed out, that the early practice of differencing arms deserves careful study, as thereby shields apparently widely different are reduced to one origin. One mode was by changing the tinctures; another, by introducing some subordinate charge; a third, by introducing a simple ordinary, as a bend, canton, bordure, or chevron. Our present duty being, however, to treat of existing arms, it may be sufficient to say, that, in a blazon of arms, Rule 8 refers usually only to a single charge used as a mark of cadency or difference; and the figures most frequently found are the crescent, mullet, martlet, fleur-de-lys, and annulet. Their usual place is in the dexter chief; or, in a quartered shield, on the fesse-point. An example is given in the crescent in the Wainwright arms, which, when fully blazoned, are "argent, on a chevron azure, a lion rampant between two fleur-de-lys of the field, all within a bordure engrailed sable, a crescent for difference."

Wainwright.

PART IV.

HERALDRY IN AMERICA.

ALTHOUGH the science of heraldry has become obsolete here, it is evident that our English ancestors brought with them the tastes and distinctions of their time and country. In all the colonies we find evidences of social distinctions, and especially of the use of those armorial insignia which are the least invidious indications of rank. Although in this chapter our examples will be mainly drawn from New England, this arises from the greater familiarity of the writer with this section of the country. It is undeniable that similar records are to be found in the Middle and Southern colonies; and, by peculiar circumstances, these latter have been supposed even to afford more examples.

This is undoubtedly an error; but the fact that heraldry was understood and practised throughout all our country is a sufficient reason for us to investigate the rules of that use.

In New England, we find a certain number of the first settlers brought with them their seals of arms, which were in common use by them. We will give the following examples from those in the first or second generation : —

Among the governors and magistrates, we find the seals of Winthrop, Bellingham, Dudley, Bradstreet, Haynes, Leete, Leverett, Coggeshall, Temple, Curwen, Lloyd, and Snelling.

These were all undeniably engraved in England, and are as follows. The reader will note that the colors are not usually marked in the engraving : —

WINTHROP: argent, three chevrons crenelé gules, over all a lion rampant sable, armed and langued azure. Crest, a hare proper, running on a mound vert. The Winthrops were from Suffolk.

Winthrop.

BELLINGHAM: sable, three bugle-horns argent. This seal bears the arms of the Lincolnshire family, and was used, in 1650, by Samuel, son of Governor Richard Bellingham ; which latter had been Recorder of Boston, county of Lincoln.

Bellingham.

DUDLEY : —— a lion rampant ——, a crescent for difference. This seal is copied from the will of Governor Thomas Dudley, in 1654. Notwithstanding much labor has been expended in England in the attempt to trace the pedigree of this Thomas Dudley, no satisfactory result has been attained. We give the seal as one portion of the evidence.

Thomas Dudley.

BRADSTREET : ——, on a fesse —— three crescents —— ; in base a hound passant. Crest, a dexter arm vambraced embowed, the hand grasping a sword. These arms are on the seal of Governor Simon Bradstreet, who was born at Horbling, county of Lincoln, in 1603, where his father, Simon, was the minister.

Bradstreet.

HAYNES : argent, three crescents barry undée, azure and gules. Crest, a stork rising, proper. Governor John Haynes was of Copford Hall, Lexden Hundred, county of Essex, and was son of John Hayes of Old-holt, in the same hundred. The Governor's descendants held the estate in 1768.

Haynes.

LEETE : argent, a fesse gules, between two rolls of matches sable, kindled proper. Crest,

three tridents erect. This is from the seal
of Governor William Leete, who had been a
Register in the Bishop's Court, at Cambridge.

LEVERETT : argent, a chevron between
three leverets running, sable. Copied from
the seal of Governor John Leverett, son of
Thomas Leverett, alderman of Boston, co.
Lincoln; in which county the family is of
great antiquity. It is probable that the
Governor was knighted by Charles II.

COGGESHALL : argent, a cross between four
escallops sable. From the seal of John Coggeshall, of Rhode Island, first president under the patent, 1647–48, secretary, &c. The
family was long seated in Essex, England.

TEMPLE : argent, two bars sable, each
charged with three martlets gold. Crest on
a ducal coronet, a martlet gold. This seal
was used by Sir Thomas Temple, a baronet
of Nova Scotia, long resident in Boston, and
much concerned in colonial affairs. He was
of the family of the present Temples, baronets, the Viscount Palmerston, &c.

CURWEN : argent, a fret ——, a chief
——; a crescent for difference. This seal
belonged to George Curwen, of Salem; and
the ring thus inscribed is represented on his
portrait, taken about 1675.

LLOYD : —— a lion rampant ——. These
arms are on the seal of James Lloyd, 1684.
He is said to have come hither from Bristol,
and enjoyed a large estate on Long Island.

SNELLING : gules, three griffin's heads
erased argent; a chief indented ermine : a
mullet for difference. This seal is from the
will of Dr. William Snelling, dated in 1674.
He describes himself as the youngest son of

Leete.

Leverett.

Coggeshall.

Temple.

Curwen.

Lloyd.

the late Thomas Snelling, of Chaddlewood, co.
Devon, at which place the family had been seated
for several generations.

Snelling.

These examples have been taken from the first
generation of settlers here. It would be easy to
extend the list greatly, but it is deemed unnecessary
to do so. We find many more examples in the
second and third generations of those born here; and, until we
are sure that there was a resident engraver capable of cutting
such seals, it is probably fair to conclude that these seals were
heirlooms, brought by the emigrants. It does not follow,
because the first generation did not leave an example of such
use, that the seals were not existing here. Personal feeling,
or any imaginable accident, might have prevented such use on
the documents remaining; and there is good reason to think,
that, among the more rigid church-members, such a use was
conscientiously avoided.

Another class of examples is to be found in our older grave-
yards. From the remaining specimens we select the following : —

WILLIAM POOLE, of Dorchester, who died in 1674. His
sister was Elizabeth Poole, the founder of Taunton, Mass.,
and, as WINTHROP says, of good family.

WILLIAM BROWNE, of Salem, who died in 1687. He is said
to have been the son of Francis Browne, of Brandon, county of
Suffolk, who was the grandson of Simon Browne, of Browne
Hall, co. Lanc.

Poole.

Browne.

JOHN LEVERETT, of Cambridge, who died in 1724, and was the grandson of the Governor already cited. His tombstone terms him "armiger."

JAMES RICHARDS, of Hartford, who died in 1680. He was an Assistant; and of his daughters, one married Governor Gurdon Saltonstall, and another married Sir John Davie, bart.

Leverett.   Richards.

Major THOMAS SAVAGE, of Boston, died in 1682. Besides this use of the arms, we find that Thomas Savage used them on his seal, as did his son and grandson.

WILLIAM STOUGHTON, of Dorchester, died in 1701. The tombstone of Governor Stoughton terms him "armiger," and the seal on his will bears the same arms. They were also used by some of his relatives here.

Savage.   Stoughton.

FRANCIS WAINWRIGHT, of Ipswich, who died in 1711. He
was the son of Francis Wainwright, who came from Chelms-
ford, England, and died here in 1692. From a seal on a deed
dated 1728, we learn that the crest of the family was a lion
rampant, holding a halbert upright.

JOHN FOWLE, of Charlestown, who died in 1711. He was
the son of George Fowle, of the same place, and was born
probably in England, about 1637.

Wainwright.

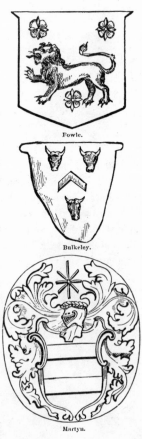

Fowle.

Bulkeley.

Martyn.

GERSHOM BULKELEY, of Weth-
ersfield, Conn., who died in 1713,
aged 77. He was the son of Rev.
Peter Bulkeley, of Concord, Mass.,
by his second wife, Grace, daughter
of Sir Richard Chetwode. Peter
was born at Odell, county of Bedford, in 1583; and was the son of
Rev. Edward Bulkeley, D.D., the
incumbent of that place, son of
Thomas Bulkeley, of Worcester,
co. Salop, descended from a family
settled at Bulclogh, co. Chester.

MARTYN, of Boston. These arms
are on a tomb, inscribed simply
with the name of Martyn; but we
find them on the seal of Michael

Martyn, in 1700, who was the only son of Richard Martyn, of Portsmouth, N.H.

To these examples, we will add a few taken from the privy seals of the governors of the colony, and used by them upon commissions and similar papers.

The seal of Sir Edmund Androsse bears a quartered coat. First and fourth : argent, on a chevron gules between three leopard's faces sable, as many castles triple-towered gold. Second and third : gules, a saltire gold, surmounted of another vert; on a chief azure, three mullets, sable. Crest, a falcon affrontant, wings expanded proper, belted gold.

Sir Edmund Androsse.

Supporters : dexter, a unicorn argent, tail cowarded ; sinister, a greyhound argent, collared gules, garnished gold.

Governor Joseph Dudley bore a lion rampant, queue fourchée ; but we do not find the tinctures.

Lieutenant-governor William Dummer, grandson of Richard Dummer, of Bishopstoke, Hants, bore azure, three fleurs-delys gold ; on a chief of the second, a demi-lion of the first. Crest, a demi-lion azure, holding in the dexter paw a fleur-delys gold.

Governor Joseph Dudley.   Lieutenant-governor William Dummer.

Governor Jonathan Belcher used on his seal the following

coat: Paly of six gold and gules, a chief vairé. Crest, a greyhound's head couped ermine, collared azure.

Governor Jonathan Belcher.

Lastly, we may here insert the arms of the Downings, Pepperrells, and Davies, all of which families were raised to the rank of baronets, as these engravings will show the manner in which the "baronet's badge" is introduced in the arms.

Pepperrell.   Davie.   Downing.

We have thus briefly indicated the principal sources of information in regard to the legitimate coat-armor of New-England families, and have given examples which will show the style of the oldest remaining examples. We have now to deal with a less agreeable portion of our task, and to point out the characteristics of the handiwork of various artists, who, during the past century, supplied our ancestors with fictitious and unfounded coats-of-arms.

So widely was this taste for drawings of arms disseminated, that, even at the present day, nearly every family of the old New-England stock possesses one or more examples; and they have often proved a serious detriment to the genealogist, by leading him to pursue a wrong line of investigation in England.

One of these herald painters who flourished in Boston prior to the Revolution was Thomas Johnson, who was born in 1708, and who died in 1767. He was an engraver, and issued several pages of music to be used with Tate and Brady's Psalms. His inventory also specifies a Book of Heraldry, valued at forty-eight shillings, from which he doubtless occasionally derived his inspiration. Herewith is inserted a copy of one of his heraldic paintings, which is signed by him, and which shows that he was capable of making a very creditable picture. In

Lynde, and others.

this particular instance, as his employer was something of an antiquary, it is most probable that the description of the arms was furnished him. The six coats here represented are those of Lynde, Newdigate, Digby, Browne, Curwen, and Smith. The escutcheon belonged to Benjamin Lynde, jr., of Salem, and is dated 1740. They are not, strictly speaking, quarterings to which he was entitled, but show alliances from which he was descended. Thus Enoch Lynde married Elizabeth Digby; their son Simon married Hannah Newdigate; whose son, Benjamin Lynde, married Mary Browne, and had Benjamin Lynde, jr. Mary Browne was daughter of William Browne and Hannah Curwen, and grand-daughter of William Browne and Sarah Smith.

Our second illustration is from a book-plate of John Franklin, brother of the famous Benjamin Franklin, and is the production of James Turner. Of this artist we have found only that he engraved a series of psalm-music, and that in 1752 he lived at Marblehead, Mass. There is as yet no way of testing the weight to be attached to his productions.

Franklin.

Probably, at even an earlier date than 1740, some of the skilful goldsmiths of the town may have painted for their employers copies of those shields which they were so often desired to chase on silver plate. There are still remaining many examples of such engraved silver; and the similarity in the form of the shields and the style of ornamentation render it probable that some of the oldest paintings had this origin.

One of the best of our Colonial engravers, and one who is

known to have been engaged on heraldic subjects, was Nathaniel
Hurd. He was born in 1729, and his family had been goldsmiths for one or two generations. He died in 1777, aged 48,
and had probably been the most prominent engraver from 1750
until his death. Quite a number of book-plates bearing coats-
of-arms, engraved by him, remain;
and in some cases, at least, the families
had a good right to display these insignia. We give here one or two
examples of these, because his peculiar form of shield is easily recognized,
as well as the delicacy of his work.

Chandler.

Sewall.

Ellery.

Next to these we place the two following cuts, which are probably the work of Hurd, or of his contemporaries.

Oliver and Fitch.

Whitmore.

The first shield is Oliver quartering Fitch and impaling Lynde. It was borne by Andrew Oliver, jr., who married Mary Lynde, in 1752. The other, the Whitmore coat, is worth a few remarks, on account of some peculiar circumstances connected with it. One of the most famous works on Heraldry, is "Gwillim's Display of Heraldrie," of which editions were published in 1611, 1632, 1638, 1660, 1679, and 1724. This might well be the standard authority of our Boston artists, and undoubtedly was in the present case. In the edition of 1660, on page 314, among the examples there given of the fretty coats, is the shield of Sir George Whitmore, Lord Mayor of London, with a mullet charged with a crescent as the difference for the second brother of the third house. In the second part, page 114, among the arms of the Knights of the Bath, is the shield of Sir Thomas Whitmore, of the same family; and the wood-cut bears a mullet for difference, though the text says he bears a crescent.

It seems quite clear, then, that the artist copied the wood-cut in the volume; and, as there was no crest in the original, he supplied the deficiency, as also two quasi-supporters. There is reason to think that some of Hurd's book-plates were copied from the same volume; at all events, they coincide with the exactness of a literal transcript.

As the result of our examination of the engravings of the artists enumerated above, it may be said, that their authority is not sufficient, when otherwise unsubstantiated, to warrant us in considering the arms as proved. We consider the English seals as *primâ-facie* evidence of a right to use arms; and we regard the Cole arms, to be soon described, as utterly worthless: the examples here described seem to occupy an intermediate position. It should be said, also, that there yet remain other evidences in the shape of embroideries and paintings by amateurs. These, of course, are of the nature of family traditions; but, when they possess any considerable antiquity, they become quite valuable witnesses.

We have lastly to speak of arms totally devoid of authority. It seems that one John Coles, of Boston, probably as early as 1776, undertook to supply all inquirers with their family arms

at a moderate cost. His name as " Heraldry painter " is in the
" Boston Directory " for 1800, and continues as late as 1813,
possibly a little later. From 1806, for some twenty years we
also find the name of John Coles, jr., a miniature and portrait
painter. It is asserted, on good authority, that the son was
engaged in the same trade ; and we have seen numerous paintings bearing a general resemblance, but apparently the work of
two individuals. We here place examples of each artist : —

It is probable that the first and more finished painting was the work of John Coles, sen., as the examples are earlier than those in the second style. These spurious paintings are easily recognized by the form of the shield, the mantlings, and palm-branches. They are widely scattered throughout New England, and are of course entirely worthless. The possessor has not always the slight satisfaction of owning a blazon of arms used by a namesake, as these artists not only patriotically granted the American flag for a crest in repeated instances, but they invented entire coats. Thus the engraving here given is a copy of an existing painting; but the arms are not recorded in any book on heraldry as used by any one of the name of Whitmore.

Lastly, in New York and Boston, and probably in other cities, seal-engravers and painters have produced innumerable coats-of-arms, all devoid of authority so far as the artists were concerned. In this country, the entire neglect of the study of heraldry may serve as a slight excuse for these assumptions : if it be any satisfaction to know that others are guilty, it is certain that in England the same unwarranted appropriations are constantly made.

It is impossible to close this section without expressing the hope that a great improvement in the use of armorial bearings will occur here. The absence of any authority competent to devise and assign new coats reduces the study of the science here to a historical investigation. Heraldry here becomes the assistant of the genealogist; and, so soon as our local historians become familiar with the signification of heraldic devices, we may expect a great addition to our knowledge of the use of arms here. With this increase of familiarity with the science, we may also expect a more scrupulous attention to its laws, and a decrease of the ridiculous assumptions which have thrown an undeserved stigma upon American heraldry.

APPENDIX.

A.

THE GORE ROLL OF ARMS.

It has become evident to those who have tried to recover the heraldic evidences remaining in New England, that seals, monumental inscriptions, and paintings, are almost the only sources of information. In Europe, in addition to all these, the investigator has the advantage of consulting the collections of many generations of heralds, forming voluminous records, wherein are depicted or described thousands of shields. In this country, we rarely find any verbal description of family arms in letters or other family documents; and hardly a single collection of a number of coats can be cited. One manuscript, however, of quite considerable antiquity, recording the bearings of numerous families in New England, was in existence recently, and is doubtless still preserved.

This document is printed in full in the "Heraldic Journal" (Boston, 1865), and has been styled the "Gore Roll of Arms." It was preserved in the family of Samuel Gore, brother of the late Governor Christopher Gore, and is said to have belonged to their father, John Gore. This John Gore, and his son Samuel, were carriage-painters in Boston in 1767, and presumably earlier. The family had been settled here for several generations. With this manuscript was inherited an English heraldic manuscript, entitled "Promptuarium Armorum," by William Smith, Rouge-Dragon, dated in 1602–1615, containing many hundred trickings of arms, which may, or may not, have been used as a reference by the Gores. The most probable explanation of this Gore collection is that it was the note-book of some painter who furnished hatchments or banners for the funerals of the persons mentioned; since such were used at that time, and the dates affixed to many of these shields coincide with the death of the bearers. At present it is impossible to trace the possession of the book beyond John Gore, born in 1718.

The original manuscript has disappeared within a few years; but it is here described from an accurate copy made by Isaac Child, Esq., a gentleman well versed in the rules of heraldry, and an accomplished draughtsman.

It has been deemed unnecessary to copy those shields which belong to foreigners; and the list comprises, therefore, only New-England coats-of-arms. The earliest coat recorded is dated in 1701, the latest in 1724: nearly all of them are confirmed by other evidences.

GORE'S LIST.

1. DEAN WINTHROP of Pulling Point, co. Suffolk, 1701.
   Argent, three chevrons gules, over all a lion rampant sable.
   Crest, on a mount vert, a hare courant ppr.

   [NOTE.— Deane was the sixth son of Governor John Winthrop, of Massachusetts, and died in 1704.]

2. RICHARD MIDCOT, of Boston, Esq., co. Suffolk. One of His Majesty's Council of the Province of Mass., 1702.
   Azure, an eagle displayed argent; on a chief gules, three escallops gold.
   Crest, a demi-eagle displayed, holding in the beak an escallop.

   [NOTE. — Richard Middlecott came from Warminster, co. Wilts, and died in 1704. BURKE gives these arms to a Lincolnshire family.]

3. ANNA, wife of PETER SARGENT, Esq., of Boston, 1702. Sargent and Shrimpton. The shield is Sargent (see No. 24) impaling argent, on a cross sable, five escallops of the field.
   Crest, a demi-lion azure, holding in his paws an escallop.

4. JOHN JAY (or Joy), of Medford, co. Middlesex, 1702.
   Argent, a chevron azure, on a chief of the second three mart-
   lets of the field.
   Crest, a cormorant's head.

5. JOHN LEGG, of Boston, Esq., co. Suffolk.
   Sable, a buck's head cabossed argent.
   Crest, out of a coronet gold, five ostrich feathers azure.

   [This family was of Marblehead.]

6. Madame ANNA LEVERIT, widow of John Leverit, Esq., Governor of the Colony of Mass., 1682.
   1st Argent, a chevron between three leverets, sable. Impaling,
   2d, Gold, on a cross gules, five bells argent.
   Crest, a scull.

   [NOTE. — The arms impaled are certainly those of Sedgewick. Savage
   says Leverett married *Sarah* Sedgewick, dau. or sister of Major Robert S.]

7. EDWARD BRATTLE, of Marblehead, co. Essex. Brattle and
   Legg, 1707.
   Gules, a chevron, gold, between three battle-axes, argent.
   Crest, a dexter arm, vambraced and embowed, grasping a battle-
   axe.
   The impalement is of the Legg arms, described in No. 5.

   [NOTE. — This Edward was a younger brother of Thomas (see No. 23),
   and married Mary, daughter of John Legg.]

8. ANNA, wife of John Richards, Esq., one of his Majesty's
   Councillors of the Province of Mass. Richards and Win-
   throp, 1707.
   Argent, four lozenges conjoined in fesse, gules, between two
   bars (sable?). Impaling, Winthrop, as in No. 1.
   No crest.

   [John Richards, who used a seal in 1685, was son of Thomas Richards,
   of Dorchester, whose widow, Welthian, also used them on her will, in
   1679.]

9. CHARLES FROST, of Boston, 1707. Frost and Davis.
   The shield is impaled, being
   1st, Frost. Argent, a chevron gules, between three trefoils
   slipped.
   2d, Davis. A stag trippant gold.
   Crest, a head, within sprigs of (laurel?).

   [This was Charles Frost, b. 1683, son of John, and grandson of Nicholas
   F., of Kittery, who was born at Tiverton, co. Devon, about 1595.]

10. NATHANIEL NORDEN, Esq., of Marblehead, one of His Majesty's
        Council.   Norden and Lat . . . . .
     Argent, on a fesse gules between three beavers passant, a cross-
        let fitchée between two fleurs-de-lys, gold.
     Crest, a demi-beaver, holding in his mouth a branch of leaves.
     The impalement is gules, a cross patonce argent.

     [This is the Latimer coat; and he married Mary, daughter of Christo-
     pher Latimer, or Lattimore, of Marblehead.   Norden died in 1727.]

11. Lady MARY, formerly wife to Sir William Phips, Knt., Gov-
        ernor of the Province of Mass., ... of Peter Sargent,
        Esq., of His Majesty's Council.   Sargent and Spencer, 1705.
     The shield is Sargent (see No. 24) impaling, Quarterly argent
        and gules — in the second and third quarters a fret gold —
        over all, on a bend sable, three escallops of the third.
     Crest, out of a ducal coronet a griffin's head, gorged with a pair
        of bars gemelles, gules, between two wings expanded.

     [NOTE. — Peter Sargent came from London, 1667; and though Savage
     does not record his first wife, she would seem to have been Anna Shrimp-
     ton.   His second wife, the widow of Gov. Phips, was daughter of Roger
     Spencer, of Saco, Maine, 1652.   Another daughter m. Dr. David Bennett,
     and had Spencer Bennett, who took the name of his uncle Phips (see
     No. 15).
          As to the Sargent arms, it may be noted that Peter used them in 1693,
     as appears by his seal on a power of attorney, now at Salem.]

12. ANTHONY CHICKLEY, Esq., Attorney-General of the Province
        of Mass., 1706.
     Azure, a chevron between three mullets, gold.
     No crest.

     [He died in 1708.   He was bapt. 31 July, 1636, at Preston-Capes,
     North-Hants, England, and was the son of William and Elizabeth Checkley.
     The same arms are on the tomb of Richard Checkley, in the Granary
     Yard, Boston.]

13. JOHN PAUL, of Boston, Mass., 1609.
     Azure, a lion rampant argent, between eight fleurs-de-lys in
        orle, gold.
     Crest, a stag's head cabossed, gules.

     [NOTE. — This is evidently the arms of John Pool, or Poole.   The
     arms are on the tomb of William Poole, of Dorchester, Mass., who d. in
     1674.]

14. Widow MARY APTHORP, widow of Charles Apthorp, of Boston, 1709.

    1st, Per pale nebuly argent and azure, in fesse two mullets, counterchanged. Impaling 2d, Quarterly, —— and ——, four eagles displayed gules.

    No crest.

15. SPENCER PHIPS, Esq., of Cambridge, co. Middlesex, one of His Majesty's Council, and Justice of the Peace for the County, 1710.

    Sable, a trefoil slipped ermine, between eight mullets, argent.

    Crest, a bear's paw, sable, holding a trefoil slipped ermine.

    [NOTE.— These arms were used by Sir William Phips (see No. 11), and very probably were granted him.]

16. JOHN FOSTER, Esq., Col. of the Life to the Earl of Bellomont, Governor of the Province of Mass., Justice of the Common Pleas for the County of Suffolk, and one of His Majesty's Council, 1710.

    Argent, a chevron vert, between three bugle-horns stringed, sable.

    Crest, a dexter arm embowed, the hand grasping a spear.

17. SUSANNAH, widow of John Foster, Esq., of Boston. Foster and Hawkins, 1710.

    1st, Foster, as in No. 22.

    Impaling 2d, Argent on a saltire sable, five fleurs-de-lys, gold.

    Crest, on a mound vert, a hind lodged ppr.

    [This seems to be an error in the Christian name. *Abigail*, dau. of Thomas Hawkins, married John Foster, and died in 1711.]

18. GURDON SALTONSTALL, Esq., Gov. of the Colony of Connecticut, 1742. Saltonstall and Whit . . . . . (Whittingham).

    1st, Gold, a bend between two eagles displayed, sable.

    Impaling 2d, Argent, a fesse (azure?) ; over all a lion rampant, gules.

    Crest, out of a ducal coronet, gold, a pelican's head, vulning its breast.

    [NOTE.— Gov. Saltonstall, son of Nathaniel, and grandson of Richard Saltonstall, jr., and Meriell Gurdon, married, for his third wife, Mary, dau- of William Whittingham, and widow of Wm. Clarke. Her grandfather was John W., who was son of Baruch W., and grandson of the distinguished Reformer, William Whittingham, Dean of Durham. Richard Saltonstall was son of Sir Richard, ambassador from England to Holland in 1644, who was nephew of Sir Richard S., Lord Mayor of London, in 1597.]

19.   SAMUEL WHITE, of Boston, merchant, 1712.
      Gules, a chevron between three boar's heads, couped argent.
      Crest, out of a mural coronet gules, a boar's head argent.

20.   WILLIAM TAYLOR, Esq., Col. of the Second Regiment of Foot,
      at the taking of the Government of Port Royal, afterward
      Lt.-Gov. of the Province, and one of the Council, 1711.
      Per saltire, gold and gules, an eagle displayed.
      Crest, a demi-eagle displayed, gules, double-headed, and in each
      beak a cross-crosslet.

      [William Taylor was the son of William Taylor, by his wife Rebecca
      Stoughton. He died in 1732. These arms were used by him on his
      seal.]

21.   ELIZABETH, wife of Simeon Stoddard, Esq., of Boston, mer-
      chant, 1712. Stoddard and Eu . . . (Evance?).
      1st, Sable, three estoiles within a bordure, argent.
      Impaling 2d, Argent, a chevron between three fleurs-de-lys,
      sable.
      Crest, a sinister arm embowed, habited gules, holding in the
      hand the stalk of a flower.

22.   GILLIS DYER, Esq., Col. of the Life-guard to his Excellency Jo-
      seph Dudley, Esq., Governor of the Province; Sheriff of
      the county of Suffolk, 1713.
      Argent, on a bend cotised azure, three crescents gold.
      Crest, a mailed arm, gauntleted, holding a dagger upright,
      hilted gold.

      [Giles Dyer died 12 August, 1713.]

23.   THOMAS BRATTLE, Esq., Treasurer of Harvard College, and
      Fellow of the Royal Society, at Boston, in the county of
      Suffolk, 1713.
      Gules, a chevron gold, between three battle-axes, argent.
      Crest, a dexter arm, embowed and vambraced, holding in the
      hand a battle-axe, gold.

      [He was the son of Thomas Brattle, of Charlestown, who died in 1683,
      the wealthiest man probably in the Colony, says Savage.]

24.   PETER SARGENT, Esq., one of His Majesty's Council for the
      Province of Mass., 1714.
      Argent, a chevron between three dolphins embowed, sable.
      Crest, a bird rising.

      [He was from London, 1667, and d. *s. p.* 1714. See No. 11.]

25. ELIZABETH, wife of Simeon Stoddard, Esq., of Boston, 1714. Stoddard and Roberts.

Stoddard impaling — Per pale argent and gules, a lion rampant, sable.

Crest, a stag's head erased, per fesse (argent and gules).

[These impalements are difficult of explanation. Simeon was son of Anthony Stoddard, and married 1st, Mary ———, who d. 1708. He m. 2d, in May, 1709, Elizabeth, widow of Col. Samuel Shrimpton, who d. April, 1713. Third, in May, 1715, Mehitable (Minot), widow of Peter Sargent. His second wife, the widow Shrimpton, was dau. of widow Elizabeth Roberts, of London.]

26. Capt. THOMAS RICHARDS, of Boston, in the county of Suffolk, 1714.

Argent, four lozenges, conjoined in fesse gules, between two bars sable.

No crest.

[This was probably the son of James Richards, of Hartford, and nephew of John R. (shield No. 8, *ante*). He died December, 1714. The tomb of James Richards, at Hartford, bears these arms.]

27. ISAAC ADDINGTON, Esq., Secretary of the Province of Mass., Judge of Probate for county of Suffolk, Justice of the Peace, and one of His Majesty's Council, 1715. Addington and Norton.

1st, Per pale ermine and erminois, on a chevron, counter-changed, four lozenges, between three fleurs-de-lys.

Impaling, Gules a fret argent, over all a bend vairy gold and gules.

Crest, a wildcat? ermine.

[Isaac Addington was son of Isaac Addington by his wife, Anne Leverett. He married, first, Elizabeth, dau. of Griffith Bowen, of London, and second, Elizabeth, widow of John Wainwright, and dau. of William Norton. She was niece of Rev. John Norton; and this branch was from the Nortons of Sharpenhow, co. Bedford. The Nortons possess an old pedigree of their family, and have used arms from the first generation here. — See also the "Herald and Genealogist" for July, 1865.]

28. ELIZABETH, wife of Elisha Cook, of Boston, Esq. Cook and Leverett, 1715.

Cook (as in No. 29) impaling Leverett (as in No. 6).

[She was daughter of Gov. John Leverett.]

29. ELISHA COOK, of Boston, Esq., one of His Majesty's Council of the Province of Mass., 1715.

Gold, a chevron chequy azu...   the field, between three cinquefoils of the second.

Crest, a unicorn's head, gold, between two wings endorsed, azure.

[Elisha Cook was son of Richard, of Boston, said to have come from Gloucestershire. He died October, 1715. His son, of the same name, married the dau. of Richard Middlecot.]

30.   ANDREW BELCHER, Esq., Commissary-General of the Province of Mass., and one of His Majesty's Council, 1717.

Gold, three pales gules, a chief vair.

Crest, a greyhound's head erased, ermine, with a collar gules, and ring (gold?).

[Andrew Belcher, a settler here in 1639, married Elizabeth, daughter of Nicholas Danforth, and had Andrew, the person here recorded, who married Sarah, daughter of Jonathan Gilbert, of Hartford. He died in October, 1717, having acquired a large fortune. His son Jonathan was the Governor of Mass. These arms are on Andrew Belcher's seal on his will.]

31.   JOSEPH LEMON, of Charlestown, in the county of Middlesex, 1717.

Azure, a fesse between three dolphins embowed, argent, an annulet for difference.

Crest, a pelican in her nest, feeding her young.

[These arms are on the family tomb, at Charlestown, Mass.]

32.   GEORGE CALDWELL, of London, merchant, now of Boston, co. Suffolk, 1717.   Caldwell and Mane.

The first coat is quarterly; viz., 1st, Per pale crenellé gules and argent, three bear's paws erased. 2nd, Three fleurs-de-lys. 3rd and 4th, Argent, a galley sable. Over all a pallet ermine.

Impaling. Per chevron flory, sable and gold, in chief three bezants, in base the stump of a tree? sable.

Crest, a hand gauntleted, holding a bear's paw erased.

[This is probably a foreign coat, the style being so different from English arms.]

33.   ELISHA HUTCHINSON, Esq., Col. of the First Regiment of Foot in the county of Suffolk, Capt. of Castle William, Chief Justice of the Court of Common Pleas in the county of Suffolk, and one of the Council, 1717.

Per pale gules and argent, a lion rampant argent, between eight crosses-crosslet gold.

Crest, out of a ducal coronet, gold, a cockatrice vert, combed gules.

[He was the son of Edward Hutchinson, of Boston, co. Linc., and of Boston, N.E. He died December, 1717. His grandson was Governor of Massachusetts.]

34. WAIGHT WINTHROP, Esq., Maj.-General of the Province of Mass., Chief Justice of the Court of Assize, and one of His Majesty's council, 1717.

Arms as No. 1. Motto, Spes vincit Thronum.

[Wait-Still Winthrop was son of Gov. John W., of Conn., and grandson of Gov. John, of Mass., hence nephew of Deane Winthrop (shield No. 1). He died November, 1717.]

35. NICHOLAS PAIGE, of Rumney Marsh, Col. of the Second Regiment of Foot, in the county of Suffolk, 1717.

Argent, on a bend, three eagles displayed.

Crest, a demi-eagle, displayed.

[He was from Plymouth, co. Devon, 1665, and married Anne, widow of Edward Lane, niece of Gov. Joseph Dudley. He died late in 1717.]

36. JOHN HUSE, Esq., of Salem, in the county of Essex, merchant, 1717.

Argent, an estoille of sixteen points, gules.

Crest, three trees proper.

37. Capt. JOHN BROWNE, of Salem, in the county of Essex, merchant, 1718.

Argent, on a bend double cotised, three eagles displayed, a crescent for difference.

Crest, an eagle displayed.

[This John Browne was grandson of William Browne, who was son of Francis Browne, of Brandon, co. Suffolk.]

38. DANIEL WIBOND, of Boston, Capt. of Marines on board His Majesty's ship Chester, 1717.

Sable, a fesse (gold?) between three swans argent, membered gules.

Crest, a dragon's head, apparently.

[These arms are those of Wyborn, co. Kent.]

39. ELIAKIM HUTCHINSON, Esq., one of His Majesty's Council for the Province of Mass., 1718.

Arms as in No. 33, but with a label of three points, argent, over all.

[Eliakim was son of Richard Hutchinson, a wealthy ironmonger of London, and cousin of Edward, of Boston. He died in 1718, probably.]

40.   JOSHUA GEE, of Boston, co. Suffolk, shipwright, 1720.   Gee and Thatcher.

1st, on a chevron, between three leopard's faces, as many fleurs-de-lys.

2d, a cross moline, on a chief three grasshoppers.

Crest, a wolf statant reguardant, ermine.

[Joshua Gee was son of Peter Gee, of Boston, 1667.   Savage seems to make some confusion in the marriages, by saying that Joshua m. Elizabeth, dau. of Rev. Thomas Thornton; but it seems that he married Elizabeth, dau. of Judah Thatcher, and gr. dau. of Thornton.   She afterwards became the third wife of Rev. Peter Thatcher, of Milton, her second cousin.

The relation was this: Thomas Thatcher, of Plymouth, Mass., was son of Rev. Peter, rector of St. Edmund's, Salisbury, co. Wilts, and nephew of Anthony; Judah was son of Anthony Thatcher, and cousin of Thomas; Rev. Peter, son of Thomas, and Elizabeth, dau. of Judah, were thus second cousins.   These Thatcher arms are confirmed by an example among the Suffolk Wills.]

41.   WIGGLESWORTH SWEETSER, of Boston, co. Suffolk, 1720.

Argent, on a fesse azure, three saltires couped, gold.

[Seth Sweetser came in 1637, aged 31, from Tring, co. Hertford.   His son Benjamin m. Abigail, probably dau. of Edward Wigglesworth, and had a son, Wigglesworth Sweetser, who had a son of the same names.]

42.   SAMUEL BROWN, Esq., of Salem, Justice of the Court of Com-Pleas, Col. of the First Regiment of Foot, co. of Essex, and one of His Majesty's Council.

Arms the same as No. 37.

[Samuel was brother of the John there recorded.]

43.   FRANCIS BRINLEY, of Newport, Colony of R.I., now of Boston, 1719.

Per pale sable and gold, a chevron between three escallops, counterchanged, all within a bordure argent, charged with eight hurts.

Crest, an escallop, gules.

[He was son of Thomas, of Datchett, co. Bucks; was of Newport, an Assistant in Rhode Island, and died in 1719.   The same arms are on the seal of Francis.]

44. JOSEPH DUDLEY, of Roxbury, co. Suffolk, Esq., Gov. of the
      Province of Mass. Bay, New England, and New Hampshire,
      1720.
      Gold, a lion rampant, azure, the tail forked.
      Crest, a lion's head erased.

      [This was the son of Gov. Thomas Dudley, whose seal bore a lion ram-
      pant, and a crescent for difference. Extended search in England has not
      yet resulted in tracing the pedigree of these Dudleys. Yet they have
      claimed and used the arms from the first generation here. We may note
      that the Dudley lion was usually *vert*, instead of azure.]

45. THOMAS CHUTE, of Marblehead, co. of Essex, 1719.
      Gules, semée of mullets gold, three swords argent, hilted gold,
      barways, the centre sword encountering the other two; a
      canton argent and azure (vert?), thereon a lion of Eng-
      land.
      Crest, a dexter cubit arm in armor, the hand grasping a broken
      sword.

      [In the " New-England Historical and Genealogical Register," xiii. 123,
      it is stated that Lionel Chute, of Ipswich, was son of Anthony Chute, and
      the descendant of Alexander Chute, of Taunton, co. Somerset, A.D. 1268.
      Lionel's son James married an Epes, of Ipswich, and had a son Thomas,
      born in 1692, the one here mentioned.
      The MS., which was then copied for the " Register," comes down only
      to this generation of Thomas Chute. It had evidently been seen by the
      author of this " Gore " list, since the arms pricked on it are those of Stur-
      ton, Bartley, Lucas, Gee, Colpepper, Baker, Wood, Brittan, and Chittester,
      which are duly entered in this list, except that Bartley, Baker, and Chit-
      tester should be Barkley, Barker, and Chichester. Mansale, which is
      found in this Roll, also occurs in the marriages.]

46. SAMUEL PHILLIPS, of Boston, co. Suffolk, 1721.
      Argent, a lion rampant, sable, collared and chained.
      Crest, a lion, as in the shield, collared and chained, gules.

      [This was very probably Samuel Phillips, goldsmith, of Salem, son of
      Rev. Samuel P., of Rowley, who was son of Rev. George P., of Boxford,
      co. Suffolk, and Watertown, Mass. George was son of Christopher Phil-
      lips, of Rainham, St. Martin, co. Norfolk, and was born about 1593.]

47. WILLIAM HUTCHINSON, Esq., of Boston, co. Suffolk, Justice of
      the Peace, 1721.
      Arms as in No. 39, but without the label, and identical with
      No. 33.

      [He was the son of Eliakim Hutchinson, and died in 1721.]

48. EDWARD PELL, of Boston, co. Suffolk, 1720. Pell and Clarke.

Quarterly, 1st and 4th, Ermine, on a canton (azure ?) a pelican vulning herself, gold.

2nd and 3rd, Gules, three swords argent, hilted gold, erect in fesse.

Crest, on a chaplet vert, a pelican, vulning herself.

[These Pell arms, and those of Pinckney, (gold, three or four fusils in bend gules,) were found on a paper, signed "John Pell and Rachael Pinckney Pell, 19 March, 1697," under the corner-stone of the church at Pelham, N.Y. The church was founded by John Pell.]

49. THOMAS SAVAGE, Esq., of Boston, Col. of the First Regiment of Foot, co. Suffolk, 1720.

Argent, six lioncels, sable.

Crest, out of a coronet, gold, a bear's paw erased, sable.

[These arms are on the tombstone of Major Thomas Savage, in the King's Chapel yard, Boston, and also on his seal. He was the son of William Savage, of Taunton, co. Somerset.]

50. ELIZABETH, wife of John Yeomans, Esq., of the Island of Antigua. Yeomans and Shrimpton. 1721.

1, Sable, a chevron between three spears upright.

2, Argent, on a cross, gold, five escallops of the field.

Crest, a dexter arm, in armor, embowed, the hand grasping a spear.

[John Yeomans was grandson of John Y., Lt.-Gov. of Antigua. Elizabeth was daughter of Samuel Shrimpton, jr., and great-granddaughter of Henry Shrimpton.]

51. ZECHARIAH TUTTLE, of Boston, co. Suffolk, Lieut. of Castle William, 1721.

Azure, on a bend argent, double cotised gold, a lion passant, sable.

Crest, a bird (Cornish chough ?) holding in its beak a branch of olive.

[These arms are those of Tothill, and are on the tomb of his brother, John T., in the Granary burying ground in Boston. Zechariah Tothill died in 1721.]

52. Mrs. ANNA WADE, of Medford, co. Middlesex, 1721.

Azure, a saltier between four escallops, gold.

Crest, a hippopotamus.

[The Wades, of Medford, were sons of Jonathan, of Ipswich, Mass., who owned lands in Denver, co. Norfolk. This Anna may be the dau. of Nathaniel Wade and Mercy Bradstreet, born in 1685.]

53. JONATHAN MOUNTFORT, of Boston, co. Suffolk, 1722.
Bendy of eight, gold and azure.
Crest, a lion's head, couped.

[In the Copp's Hill yard, in Boston, is found the same coat on the
Mountfort tomb, bearing date of 1724.   Edmund, Henry, and Benjamin,
brothers, are said to have come here in 1656 and 1675.]

54. DANIEL STODDARD, a naval officer of the Port of Boston,
1723.
Sable, three estoilles within a bordure argent, a crescent for
difference.
Crest, a demi-horse ——, erased, environed round the body with
a coronet, gold.

55. Widow of Joseph Dudley, Esq., of Roxbury, co. Suffolk, 1722.
1st, Gold, a lion rampant (azure ?).   Impaling, —— on a bend
double cotised, three martlets.
Crest, a wolf's head, erased.

[This is evidently Rebecca, daughter of Edward Tyng, and wife of
Gov. Joseph Dudley. She survived her husband, and died September,
1722. These arms of Tyng are on old plate, still preserved in the family.
See also No. 60.]

56. MARY, widow of Francis Brinley, of Newport, in the Colony of
Rhode Island.   Brinley and Borden, 1722.
1st, Per pale argent and gold, a chevron between three escallops, counterchanged, within a bordure argent, charged with
eight hurts.   (See No. 43.)   Impaling, argent, three cinquefoils, azure.
Crest, an escallop gules.

57. JOHN JEKYLL, of Boston, Esq., Collector of the Customs for
the Counties of Suffolk, Middlesex, Plymouth, Barnstable,
and Bristol, 1723.
Gold, a fesse between three hinds trippant, sable.
Crest, a horse's head couped argent, maned and bridled, sable.

58. BENJAMIN PICKMAN, Esq., of Salem, co. Essex, 1723.
Gules, two battle-axes in saltire gold, between four martlets,
argent.
No crest.

[Benjamin Pickman, of Salem, says Savage, was third son of Nathaniel,
of Bristol, Eng., where he was baptized at Lewen's Mead (Bristol), in
1645; had a son Benjamin, who died in 1718, leaving a son Benjamin,
born 1708. These arms are also in the Salem churchyard.

59. WILLIAM DUMMER, Esq., of Boston, co. Suffolk, Lt.-Gov. of the Province of Mass., one of the Council, and Capt. of Castle William, 1723.

Azure, three fleurs-de-lys gold, on a chief of the second, a demi-lion of the field.

Crest, a demi-lion azure, holding in the dexter paw a fleur-de-lys, gold.

[These arms are used by Gov. Dummer on his official privy seal. He was grandson of Richard Dummer, of Bishopstoke, Hants.]

60. JONATHAN TYNG, Esq., of Woburn, co. Middlesex, Col. of the Second Regiment of Foot, Justice of the Court, 1724.

Argent, on a bend cotised sable, three martlets, gold.

No crest.

[He was son of Edward Tyng, and died in January, 1724. The family was one of the most prominent in Massachusetts, and was connected by marriage with many of the families already noted as using arms. See No. 55.]

61. JAMES TILESTONE, of Boston, co. Suffolk, 1724.

Azure, a bend cotised between two garbs, gold.

Crest, out of a mural coronet gules, a greyhound's head.

[These are the arms of Tillotson, of which name this is probably a corruption.]

62. JOHN FRIZELL, of Boston, merchant. Frizell and Fowle.

First, Quarterly, 1st and 4th, Argent, three antique crowns, gules.

2nd and 3rd, Azure, three cinquefoils, argent.

Impaling, Argent, three trees proper.

Crest, a stag's head, between two halberts.

[These arms of Frizell or Frazer are also on a silver flagon, given by John F. to the Second Church in Boston. He d. in 1723.]

63. RICHARD WALDRON, Esq., of Portsmouth, in Piscatequa, alias New Hampshire, 1724.

Argent, three bull's heads cabossed, horned gold.

64. BOARLAND.

Argent, two bars, gules, over all a boar rampant (azure ?).

Crest, a broken lance.

Motto, Press Through.

[John Borland, of Boston, used these arms on his seal. He died in 1727. His brother Francis was of Glasford, North Britain.]

65. CUSHING.

Quarterly, 1st and 4th, An eagle displayed.

2nd and 3rd, Two dexter hands open, couped, a canton chequy.

Crest, two bear's paws, holding a ducal coronet, from which is suspended a heart.

[No colors or individual owner are marked on this sketch. The family, however, is a distinguished one here, and the pedigree will be found in the "New-England Historical and Genealogical Register" for 1865.]

66. JOSHUA WINSLOW, Esq.

Argent, on a bend gules eight lozenges conjoined, gold.

Crest, the stump of a tree.

[More correctly, the bend should be gules, lozengy gold; but it is given as it is painted. The Winslows, a family which gave two governors to the Plymouth Colony, have used these arms on many occasions. Their tomb, in the King's Chapel yard, in Boston, bears this coat.]

67. SAYWARD, of York.

Gules, on a fesse argent, between two chevrons ermine, three leopard's faces of the field.

Crest, a tiger's head, couped.

[Henry Sayward was of York, Me., 1664.]

68. Argent, a chevron gules between three pine-apples, vert, on a canton a fleur-de-lys, in the centre point a baronet's badge.

Crest, out of a ducal coronet a mailed arm embowed, the hand grasping a staff; thereon a flag.

Mottos, "Peperi" and "Virtute."

[These arms, though not clearly emblazoned, are certainly those of Sir William Pepperell, Bart. It is very probable that he inherited the arms, and that the canton is an augmentation. The baronetcy is now extinct.]

69. BELL, of Boston.

Azure, a fesse ermine, between three bells, gold.

[It should be mentioned, that the last five coats are not finished in the drawing, and the names of the owners are not all specified.]

70. CHRISTOPHER KILBY, Esq.

Argent, three bars azure, in chief as many annulets of the last.

Crest, an ear of maize, stripped open (ppr. ?).

Mottos, "Persisto," and "Gratia Gratiam Parit."

71. GILBERT MCADAMS. McAdams, Kilby, and Clark.

Gules, three crosses-crosslet fitchée, argent.

On an escutcheon of pretence Kilby (as in No. 70), quartering Clarke; viz., a bend raguly and trunked, between three roundles.

[Christopher Kilby, son of John, married Sarah, daughter of Hon. John Clarke, and had an only daughter, Sarah, who married Gilbert McAdams. Christopher Kilby acquired a large estate, and lived at Betchworth, co. Surrey, where he died in 1771.]

B.

FOR the purpose of comparison, the following list of heraldic terms in French and Latin is reprinted from Planché's edition of Clark's "Introduction to Heraldry," London, 1866.

AN ALPHABETICAL

LIST OF HERALDIC TERMS,

IN

ENGLISH, FRENCH, AND LATIN.

English.	French.	Latin.
ABATEMENT	Abatement	Diminutiones armorum
Addorsed	Addossé	
Adumbration		Adumbratio
Alerions	Aiglettes, Aiglons	Aquilæ Mutilæ
Anchored	Ancré	Anchoratus
Annulet	Annelet	Annulus, vel Annellus
Argent	Argent	Argenteus
Armed	Armé	Armatus
Armoury, Armory	Armoiries	Insignia
Attired	Acorné	
Avelane		Crux Avellana
Azure	Azur	Asureus
Bar	Barre	Vectis
Bar-Gemel	Jumelles	Jugariæ fasciolæ
Barrulet	Barelle	Barrula
Barruly	Barellé	Transverse fasciolatus
Barry	Fascé	Fasciatum
Barry Pily	Parti Emanché	Runcinatus
Barry-per-pale	Contreface	Contrafasciatus
Barbed and Crested	Barbé et Cresté	Barbula et Crista

English.	French.	Latin.
Barnacles		Pastomides
Barnicle		Bernicla
Baton	Baston	Bacillus
Beaked	Becqué	Rostratus
Bend	Bande	Tænia
Per Bend Sinister	Contrebarré	Contravittatus
Bendy	Bandé	Bendulatus
Bendy of Six	Contrebandé	
Bend Sinister	Barre	Vitta
In bend	En Bande	Oblique dextrorsus positus
Party-per-bend	Tranché	Oblique dextrorsus biparti-tum
Bendlet	Bandelette	Bandula
Bezant	Besant	Bizantius nummus
Bezanty	Bezanté	
Billets	Billettes	Laterculi
Billetty	Billetté	Laterculatus
Border	Bordure	Fimbria
Bordered	Bordé	Fimbriatus
Caboshed	Cabossé	Ora obvertantia
Caltraps	Chaussé-trappes	Murices or Tribuli
Canton	Canton	Quadrans Angularis
Cantoned	Cantonnée	Stipatus
Charge	Charge	Figura
Charged	Chargé	Ferens
Checky	Echiqueté	Tesselatum
Chess-Rook		Lusorius Latrunculus
Chevron	Chevron	Cantherius
Per Chevron	Mantelé	Manteliatum
Chevrony	Chevroné	Cantheriatus
Chief	Chef	Summum
In Chief	In Chef	In Summo
Cinquefoil	Quinquefeuille	Quinquefolia
Cleché	Cleché	Floralus
Close	Clos	Clausum
Collared	Acollé	
Combatant	Affronté	Pugnantes
Compony	Componé	Compositus
Counter-Compony	Contre Componé	
Counterchanged	Parti de l'un en l'autre	Transmutatus
Counter-imbattled	Bretessé	Utrinque-pinnatus
Counter-quartered	Cont'-Escartelé	Contraquadrate partitus
Counter-potent	Contrepotencé	Partibulatum
Counter-Vair	Contrevaire	
Coward	Couée	
Cotice	Cotice	Tæniola
Cotised	Cotové	Utroque latere accinctus
Couchant	Couchant	Jacens

English.	French.	Latin.
Couped	Coupé	A latere disjunctum
Combed	Cresté	
Couple-close		Cantheria
Courant	Courant	Currens
Crowned	Couronnée	Coronatus
Crescent	Croisant	Luna Cornuta
Crest	Crête	Crista
Crested	Cresté	
Cross	Croix	Crux
In Cross	En Croix	In modum crucis collocata
Crosslet	Croisette	Crucicula
Dancette	Danché	Denticulatus
Defamed	Diffamé	
Demy	Demi	Dimidiatus
Diapered	Diapré	Duriatus
Differences	Brisures	Diminutiones armorum
Displayed	Eployé	Expansus
Dismembered	Dismembré	
Dismembred	Morné	Mutilatus
Dormant	Dormant	Dormiens
Doublings	Doublé	
Dove-Tail	Assemble	
Embattled	Crenelé	Pinnatus
Engrailed	Engrailé	Striatus
Engrafted	Enté	Insitus
Environed	Environé	Septus
Erased	Arraché	Lacer
Eradicated		Eradicatus
Ermine	Hermines	
Ermines	Contre Hermines	
Escalop	Coquille	Conchilium
Escarbuncle	Escarboucle	Carbunculus
Escutcheon	Ecusson	Scutum
Etoile	Etoile	Stellula
Fess	Face	Fascia
Per Fess	Coupé	Transverse sectum
Fitchy	Fiché	Figibilis
Fillet	Filet	
Fimbriated	Franché	Fimbriatus
Flanch	Flanque	Orbiculi segmentum
Flory	Florence	Liliatus
Fret	Frette	Frectum simplex
Fretty	Fretté	Frectata
Furs	Pannes	Pellis
Fusil	Fusée	Fusus
Fusilly	Fuselé	Fusillatum
Garb	Gerbe	Fascis frumentarius
Galtrap	Chaussée-trappe	Murices

English.	French.	Latin.
Gardant	Gardante	Obverso ore
Gliding	Ondoyante	Undans
Gorged	Clariné	Cymbalatus
Gules	Gueules	Ruber
Gutty	Gutté	Guttis respersum
Gyron	Gyron	Cuneus
Gyronny	Gironné	Cuneatus
Hauriant	Hauriant	Hauriens
Helmet	Casque	Galea
Horned	Accorné	
Hooded	Chapperoné	Calyptratus
Imbattled	Crenellé	Pinnatus
Indented	Danché	Indentatus
Incensed	Animé	Incensus
Indorsed	Adossé	Ad invicem tergum vertentes
Inescutcheon	Ecusson	Scutulum
Ingrailed	Engraillé	Striatus
Invecked	Canellé	Invectus
Issuant	Issant	Nascens
Label	Lambel	Lambella
Lambrequin	Lambrequin	Pennæ
Langued	Lampasse	Lingua
Lozenge	Lozange	Rhombus
Lozengy	Lozangé	Rhombulis interstinctus
Mantle	Manteau	Pallium
Martlet		Merula
Manche	Manche	Manica
Mascle	Macle	Macula
Masoned	Massoné	Glutinatus
Membred	Membré	Tibiatus
Millrind	Fer de moulin	Ferrum molendinarium
Montant	Montant	Resupinus
Mound	Monde	Mundus
Musseled	Emmuselé	
Mullet	Molette	Rotula Calcaris
Nebuly	Nebulé	Nubilatum
Or	Or	Aurum
Orle	Environné	Limbus
In Orle	Environné	Ad oram positus
Over all	Sur le tout	Toti superinductum
Pale	Pal	Palus
In-pale	En Pal	In Palum collocatus
Pall	Pairle	
Paly	Pallé	Palis exoratus
Palet	Vergetté	Palus minutus
Paly-per-fess	Contrepalé	Contrapalitus
Party-per-pale	Parti	Partitus

English.	French.	Latin.
Papillone	Papellonné	Papillionatus
Passant	Passant	Gradiens
Patty	Paté	Patens
Paw	Patte	
Perished	Peri	
Pheon	Fer de dard	Ferrum jacul
Pile	Pointe	Pila Pontis
Pometty	Pometté	Sphærulatus
Potent	Potence	Patibulatum
Proper	Propre	Color naturalis
Purpure	Pourpre	Purpureus color
Quarter	Quartier	Quadrans
Quarterly	Escartelé	Quadripartite
Quartering	Escarteler	Cumulationes armorum
Quarterly Quartered	Contre escartelent	
Quatrefoil	Quatrefeuille	Quatuorfolia
Rampant	Rampant	Erectus
Ranged	Rangé	Ordinatus
Rebuses	Armes parlantes	
Reversed	Renversé	
Regardant	Regardant	Retrospiciens
Respectant	Affronté	Pugnantes
Rising	Essortant	Surgens
Rompu	Rompu	Fractus
Roundle	Torteau	Tortella
Sable	Sable	Ater, or Niger
Saltier	Sautoir	Decussis
Party-per-Saltire	Escartelé en sautoir	
Saltirewise	Posé en sautoir	In decussim dispositum
Saliant	Saillant	Saliens
Scaled	Escaillé	
Segreant	Segrant	Erectus
Sejant	Assis	Sedens
Seme	Semé	Sparsus
Shortened	Raccourci	Accisus
Streaming	Chevelée	
Stringed	Enguiché	Appensus
Statant	En pied	
Surmounted	Surmonté	
Tail	Queue	Cauda
Taloned	Onglé	Ungulatus
Tierce	Tierce	Tertiatum
Treille	Treillé	
Trefoil	Treffle	Trifolium
Tripping		More suo incedens
Trunked	Tronqué	Truncatus
Tusked	Defendu	
Vair	Vairé	Variegatum

English.	French.	Latin.
Vert	Vert	Viridis color
Voided	Vuidé	Evacuatus
Volant	Volant	Volans
Vorant	Engoulant	Vorans
Umbrated	Ombré	Inumbratus
Water Bouget	Bouse	Uter Aquarius militaris
Wavy	Ondé	Undulatus
Whirlpool	Tournant d'Eau	Gurges
Two Wings expanded	Vole	Ala
A Wing	Un Demi Vol	Ala simplex
Winged	Aislé	Alatus
Wreath	Torce	Tortile
Wyvern	Dragon	Viverra

INDEX.